FIGURE SKATING
Championship Techniques

Sports Illustrated Winner's Circle Books

BOOKS ON TEAM SPORTS

Baseball
Basketball
Football: Winning Defense
Football: Winning Offense
Hockey
Lacrosse
Pitching
Soccer

BOOKS ON INDIVIDUAL SPORTS

Bowling
Competitive Swimming
Cross-Country Skiing
Figure Skating
Golf
Racquetball
Skiing
Tennis
Track: Championship Running

SPECIAL BOOKS

Canoeing
Fly Fishing
Scuba Diving
Strength Training

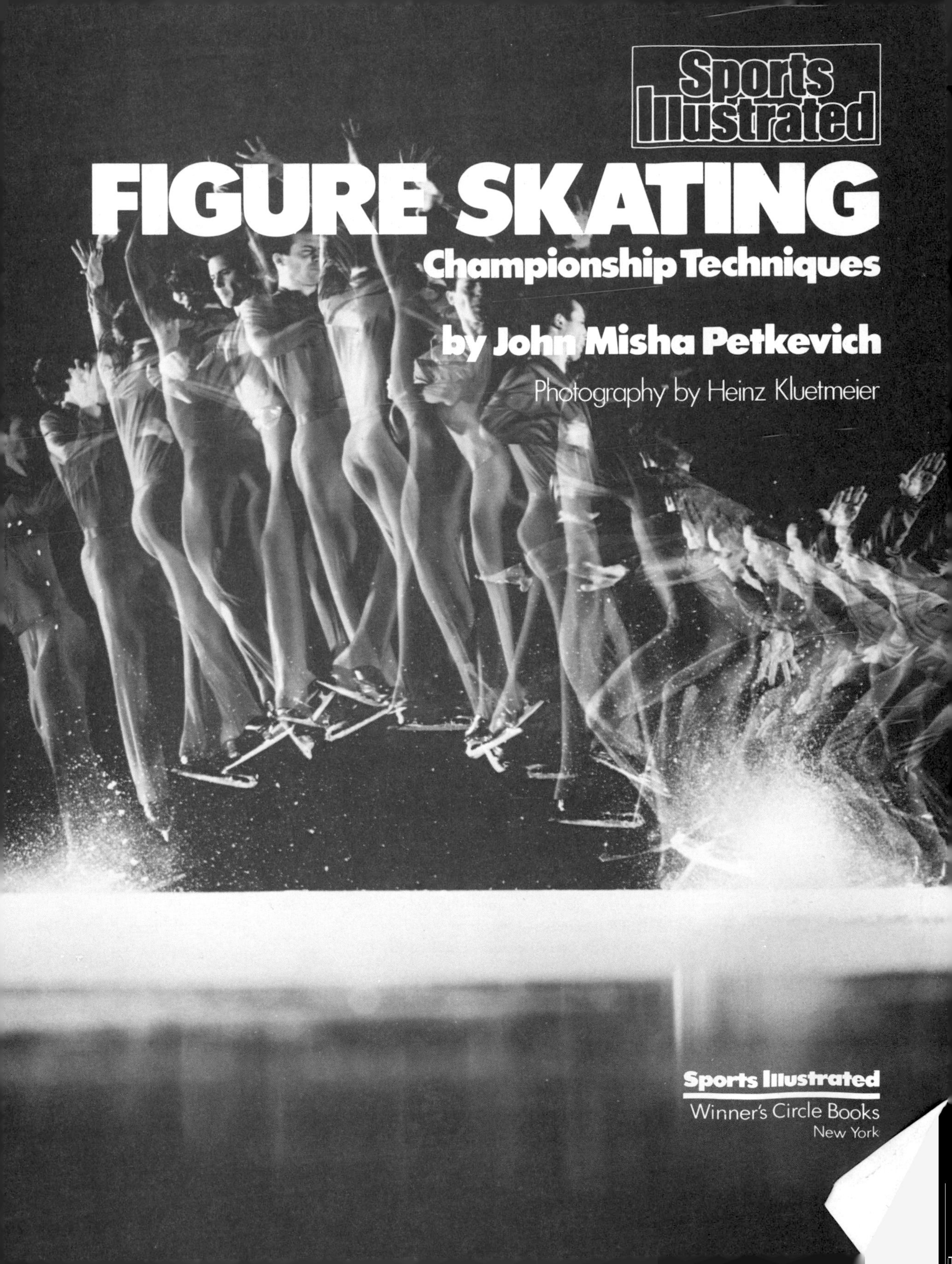

Sports Illustrated

FIGURE SKATING
Championship Techniques

by John Misha Petkevich

Photography by Heinz Kluetmeier

Sports Illustrated
Winner's Circle Books
New York

In memory of a great woman of figure skating,
my mother.

Picture Credits: Page 10 Author's collection; 269 by William Udell. For *Sports Illustrated:* Pages 14, 24, 36, 176, 270 by Richard Mackson; 20 (upper right), 156, 190, 282, 284 by Manny Millan; 20 (bottom) by Ronald C. Modra; 126, 134, 181, 278 bottom by Bill Eppridge; 185 by Jerry Cooke; 278 (top) by Eric Schweikardt, 281 by Tony Tomsic. Cover and all other photographs by Heinz Kluetmeier.

FIRST EDITION

Designer: Kim Llewellyn

Library of Congress Cataloging-in-Publication Data

Petkevich, John Misha.
    Sports illustrated figure skating: championship techniques/by John Misha Petkevich; photography by Heinz Kluetmeier.—1st ed.
        p.   cm.—(Sports illustrated winner's circle books)
    ISBN 0-452-26209-7
        1. Skating.   I. Sports illustrated (Time, inc.)   II. Title.
III. Title: Figure skating.   IV. Series.
GV850.4.P48   1988
796.91—dc19   88-18597
    ISBN 0-452-26209-7 (pbk.)   89 90 91 92 AG/HL 10 9 8 7 6 5 4 3 2 1

Contents

8

FIGURE SKATING

Championship Techniques

Introduction

Writing this book has been one of the most enjoyable experiences I have ever had. As I wrote, I was able to relive all the sensations and experiences of my own skating career. This has been particularly important to me for the following reasons:

First, I simply loved to skate, and I have always relished any opportunity to revisit skating.

Second, I made a decision in 1972, following the Olympic Games and the World Championships, to leave skating and to devote my energies to new endeavors. I knew that my many other interests would permit me only enough time to maintain the level of skating expertise I had achieved. Since I was interested in improvement as a skater, not just maintenance, a clean break from skating was the only solution. I returned to the ice only on very special occasions. Although I have remained in close contact with the sport as a television commentator, advisor, coach, and founder of "An Evening with Champions" (a skating show at Harvard University that raises money for The Dana Farber Cancer Foundation), working on this book gave me the chance to immerse myself in skating once again.

Finally, I wanted to share my insights into skating technique with future skaters. This knowledge has developed over many years of analyzing skating and consulting with some of the best technicians in the sport, and represents a distillation of the many theories and practices prevalent in the skating world. It is, I hope, a compilation of the best, most up-to-date techniques derived from the basic physical principles that have always governed figure skating.

The author practicing what he preaches, as a competitive figure skater in 1966.

A WORD OF THANKS

Many people have contributed to this book—some directly, others indirectly. To name all of those who have had some influence would require another volume, and I would inevitably leave someone out. So, I shall mention only those individuals who have had a direct involvement in the book, or whose theories and techniques are found throughout its text.

The two coaches who exerted the greatest influence on my understanding of technique were Arthur Bourque, my coach during the peak years of my skating career, and Gustav Lussi, my technical consultant during the final 18 months of my amateur skating career. Arthur taught me the basics as well as how to leap higher than I thought possible, plus the benefits of drive, persistence, and training. He stood by me through the last eight years of my career and allowed me to consult with other coaches regarding their approach to technique. Gus, on the other hand, taught me the fundamental physical principles of skating and how to apply them. He encouraged analysis and thought. Although my time with Gus was brief, it was full and thorough. His 30-year contribution to skating in general was immense.

My skating career would not have been possible without the support of my parents. They made many sacrifices to provide me with the opportunities to develop my talents; their limitless selflessness is a tribute to them and a sterling example to others. True love of parent for child could not be expressed in a more poignant way.

With respect to writing this book, several individuals have been most helpful. Tracie Brown, whose picture appears throughout the book, took time out of her hectic training schedule to execute many of the basic moves described and illustrated here. Her impeccable line and style made the photography session a delight. Brian Boitano, the 1988 Olympic Gold Medalist, performed the most difficult maneuvers in figure skating during a photographic session. Even the quadruple toe loop is included in the book. Without the talent of Heinz Kluetmeier, the man with the magic sports-photo lens, the beauty and precision of Tracie and Brian could not have been captured. His magnificent photos have been incorporated for nearly all of the instructional segments of the book. Benjamin T. Wright contributed a great deal of information and perspective on the historical aspects of skating. Bill Jaspersohn, my editor, has been encouraging, understanding, and insightful. His clear vision for the book provided the guiding light. My faithful secretary, Cathy Barlow, did wonders with my copious notes, corrections, inserts, and amendments.

Finally, *Sports Illustrated Figure Skating: Championship Techniques* would not have materialized without the loving understanding of my family. Throughout vacations and during my spare time after long work hours, I became a prisoner of the thoughts contained here. My wife, Mary, gracefully endured many quiet nights and several virtually conversationless vacations. My beautiful children, Jonathan, Lisa, and Michelle, allowed me to be absent from their side without any diminution in their love and affection. Michelle has gone so far as to incorporate the techniques contained in this book in her own skating, providing me with an ideal empirical model. In the end, family teamwork produced this work.

FOR THE LOVE OF IT

There is only one good reason to learn how to skate, and that is for the sheer fun of it. Certainly you may have other reasons, quite good ones in fact; but if you don't love the idea of gliding on ice, if you are not thrilled by the thought of leaping into the air, or if the image of a cold wind biting your cheeks as you fly around the rink does not send welcome shivers up your spine, then skating is not for you. If you start skating in search of its pleasures and thrills, you'll find unimagined fulfillment.

I can vividly remember my first few years on the ice, when I was hardly an example of a disciplined and goal-oriented skater. For me it was fun and games: the speed, the feeling of jumping and rotating in the air, and—believe it or not—the sensation of falling.

During my early years, my main concern was to have a good time. I would try anything; fear or uncertainty had no place. A lot of effort went into each attempt, but little thought or knowledge backed up my efforts. Through the daring, the physical effort, and the fun ran a thread of ambition and desire. Later, when the awareness and discipline of technique became a part of my skating, the love of it had already built the foundation. And it was on this foundation that I was able to build a skating career.

My experiences are not unique. Dick Button, two-time Olympic Gold Medalist and well-known sports commentator, attributes his continuing involvement in the world of figure skating to his love of the sport. You have only to see Dr. Tenley Albright, the 1956 Olympic Gold Medalist, on the ice even now to realize how profoundly she loves skating. Most champions convey this sentiment.

However, a love of skating is not exclusive to champions or to champion-

His passionate love of skating helped make Brian Boitano an Olympic champion.

ship material. Enthusiasm comes in many forms—such as when a young beginner ends a practice session happier than when he or she began, and wants to practice longer. For those who truly love it, figure skating can be mastered without difficulty.

If you share this enthusiasm, then skating is for you. So . . . let's go!

Key to Diagrams

Below is a listing of the abbreviations in the diagrams that appear throughout this book.

RFI	=	Right forward inside edge
LFI	=	Left forward inside edge
RBI	=	Right back inside edge
LBI	=	Left back inside edge
RFO	=	Right forward outside edge
LFO	=	Left forward outside edge
RBO	=	Right back outside edge
LBO	=	Left back outside edge

1

Some Preliminaries

Before jumping onto the ice, you must make a few decisions. First, where are you going to skate? And who will teach you? Finding the answers may be more complicated than you might anticipate.

The first step to answering these questions is to identify your goal: What kind of skater do you want to be? Do you want to be a casual skater, gliding around an outdoor pond two or three times a year? Or do you want to be the kind of recreational skater who can gracefully maneuver around a packed skating rink on Friday nights, able to execute simple maneuvers but not skilled enough to attempt any fancy jumps or spins. Perhaps you aspire to become an Olympian, to represent your country at the Olympic Games. Or you may see skating as a professional pursuit, meaning that the skills you learn will be critical to your ability to make a living in the future.

Once you determine your goal, you may have to face the fact that achieving it will require some sacrifices. Ice time is not always readily or conveniently available—a skating rink may not be near at hand, or its hours may be limited. (Few school districts have skating rinks.) This may mean traveling a good distance to practice. The decision to become a certain type of skater brings with it certain requirements, and to make the journey to that goal as easy as possible, it's best to resolve at the outset to take the steps necessary to achieve it.

Needless to say, these questions are virtually impossible to answer before you have even stepped onto the ice. How can you know if you haven't tried it? As luck would have it, you don't have to identify your goals instantly and irrevocably. In fact, your goals are likely to change as you develop as a skater. However, if you are able to identify your objectives correctly early on, the road to your goal will have fewer detours and you will experience a greater probability of success.

17

No matter what their age, serious skaters need quality instruction. Here, former World Champion Cecilia Colledge passes on her years of experience and accumulated knowledge to a young pupil.

WHERE

The least difficult of these questions at the beginning is *where*. Where will you skate? More often than not, where you skate is dictated by where you live. For example, where I grew up, in Great Falls, Montana, your choices were limited to two. Either you skated on Gibson Pond, an outdoor pond on whose ice I set foot for the first time at the ripe young age of two, or you skated in the Civic Center, the only indoor rink in the area (a new arena, the Four Seasons, has since superseded the Civic Center). In Great Falls, the skater wanting a couple of outings per year for exercise, and the enjoyment of the brisk winter air in Montana, would undoubtedly opt for Gibson Pond. However, the skater looking for the opportunity to skate seriously, to progress as rapidly as possible, and to practice daily would choose the Civic Center.

A different set of alternatives would be available to skaters living in, say, Greenwich, Connecticut. Several rinks are within an hour's drive of Greenwich, each offering schedules suitable to skaters with different objectives. Both the number and type of alternatives are numerous.

Wherever you live, the principal factors in making the decision about where to skate are the location, the type of rink (indoor or outdoor), the amount of time available for the kind of skating you intend to pursue, the type of programs offered, and the quality of the coaching staff. The higher your goal, the more time you will require and the more stable the conditions must be. Therefore, if you aspire to be an Olympian, an indoor rink offering long hours of practice will provide your best option.

PROGRAMS

A wide range of instructional programs for the casual, recreational, serious, and competitive skater is generally available at most rinks. No matter what your goals and needs, programs exist to address your requirements. Most of these are organized by the different skating organizations (more on that in a moment). Since your objectives will ultimately determine the skating organization that you join, it is essential to consider both organization and program together when evaluating the different instructional programs.

In the United States, both the United States Figure Skating Association (USFSA) and the Ice Skating Institute of America (ISIA) offer extensive programs for learning how to skate. The fundamental difference between the USFSA and the ISIA lies in the objectives of the members. For the USFSA, the objective is to nurture the development at all levels leading ultimately to participation in Olympic and World Competitions. Therefore it is the official national governing body recognized by the International Skating Union (ISU) and the International Olympic Committee. The ISIA, the trade association of rink owners and operators, is dedicated to bringing skating skills to the widest possible group of people, and besides hosting competitions for skaters of all levels of expertise, it attempts to provide a program in which skaters can learn skating as a profession.

INSTRUCTION

It's certainly no secret that instruction reduces the time required to learn a new sport. Not surprisingly, then, several different types of skating instruction have arisen, making the question of what kind of instruction an important one.

Basically, three different forms of instruction are available in figure skating: group, semi-private, and private. The more experienced a skater you are, the greater will be your emphasis on private lessons. The less experienced you are, the greater will be the emphasis on group instruction. Generally, a skater starts with group lessons and progresses to private lessons; occasionally semi-private lessons serve as an intermediate step or as a supplement to group or private lessons. This is, of course, an oversimplification. For a more detailed explanation, as well as further information on rinks, skating organizations, and programs, see my earlier book, *The Skater's Handbook* (New York: Charles Scribner's Sons, 1984).

With respect to many of the more advanced moves described in this book, it is important to seek professional assistance. As in any sport, athletes can sustain injury as they attempt to advance their expertise. These moves should be learned with the help of an instructor.

THE EVENT

At some point during the learning process, you will be faced with making a decision about which discipline to pursue. There are three choices: singles, pairs, and ice dancing. Your choice of a particular discipline depends first and foremost on your interests. In addition, it is worth considering other factors, such as your physical stature and skating strengths, and the availability of coaching for a particular discipline. Often, you will make the decision before

Singles skating.
Singles skating consists of two disciplines: compulsory figures (left) and free skating (right). In the future, compulsory figures may be eliminated from all competitions.

Pairs skating.
Pairs skaters need strong singles-skating skills to be successful.

Ice dancing.
In ice dancing, athleticism is the servant of beauty.

you have the answer to all the relevant questions. In any case, you should be aware of the important elements of each discipline.

In singles skating, a skater must pursue two disciplines: compulsory figures and free skating. The compulsory figures are variations on the basic figure eight. Currently, sentiments in the U.S. are building to eliminate compulsory, or school figures as they're called, from competition. The ISU has already moved to eliminate compulsory figures from all international skating competitions beginning July 1, 1990. Resistance to this move in the U.S. has been based on the erroneous belief that compulsory figures teach the skater good basic technique. This is incorrect, since the techniques suitable for figures are totally different from those required for free skating. In addition, any of the edges and turns learned in compulsory figures can as easily, if not more efficiently, be learned with defined free-skating exercises. The elimination of the compulsory figures will give figure skating a dramatic boost. At the very least, skaters will have more time to concentrate on free skating (which is unquestionably the more athletic, artistic, and from the spectator's perspective, appealing aspect of singles skating). In competition, free skating consists of two parts: an original program, a 2-minute, 40-second program of required elements that tests technical expertise; and the long or "free-skating" program, which is the synthesis of the skater's technical and artistic capabilities.

Pairs is essentially a free-skating event. In competition, pair skating, like singles, has two parts—an original and a free-skating program. A brief chapter at the end of the book describes several elements unique to pair skating.

Ice dancers compete in three different disciplines. Compulsory dances are dances for which the sequence of steps, the partner holds, the music, and sometimes the exact pattern created on the ice are prescribed. The second element is the original set pattern dance. This is similar to a set pattern compulsory dance except that the dance consists of steps of the couples' own invention to a tempo and rhythm prescribed in advance. The third element is the free dance, which, like free skating, is a synthesis of the skaters' athletic and artistic ability and a true test of musicality.

EQUIPMENT

Before you can set foot on the ice, two items of equipment are required: skates and the appropriate clothing. For skaters of all levels, the choices of skates and clothing take some consideration.

A properly laced skating boot—snug at the toe, loose at the instep, and firm but not too snug at the top—can improve your chances of having a pleasurable time on the ice.

Skates

If you don't own a pair of skates, then it is essential that you give some thought to the type of skates to purchase.

As a general rule, you should purchase a skate that has enough support around the ankle to keep it from flopping from side to side, but not so much that the stiffness could precipitate a serious leg injury by preventing you from bending the ankle and knee adequately. The skate should border on the uncomfortable but not actually be uncomfortable. If you have ever worn a ski boot, you will probably find a skating boot as soft as kid gloves—though not quite as smoothly lined or as roomy. Even more important than the degree of stiffness around the ankle is the fit of the boots. Boots fit properly if they are snug yet relatively comfortable, with adequate room at the toes.

For the beginner, a skate blade known as a combination style is best. This blade can be used for all the techniques that the relatively inexperienced skater is likely to confront. As you gain expertise, your needs will become more specific and more varied. For example, there are blades designed specifically for compulsory figures, for free skating, and for ice dancing, and there are many different types within each category.

Regardless of the type of blade, you will need guards to wear on them when you are walking around off the ice. These protect the skating surface of the blade. (Blades should be treated the same way you would a good knife, the cutting edge being fragile and sensitive to impact against an unyielding surface like cement or pebbles.)

The Skater's Handbook delineates in detail the kinds of skates available, the relative cost of each type, the kind of skate appropriate to the level of expertise, and where they can be obtained.

Clothing

Most of us agree that skating is both athletic and artistic. Therefore, the clothing you choose for skating should display both of these aspects to the best advantage. Athletically, you want the observer to be able to see your technique and prowess. Artistically, you want to show off your beauty and theatricality. To accomplish this, your clothing should reveal your body line yet allow you to move freely. At the same time, the temperature of the rink in which you are skating, a factor which can vary greatly from one to the next, will have an impact on your choices. Here are some guidelines:

- For the beginner, the primary consideration is warmth. Just make sure that the clothing is stretchy or sufficiently loose. If it is neither, the outfit will feel confining and may even hamper your progress.
- When you try on clothing in a store, take the time to find out just how much you can move in it. Lift your legs and arms as far as you can in every direction; do back bends and touch your toes. Squat. If the clothes don't prevent you from doing any of these movements comfortably, then you've got what you need.
- The present craze in exercise wear will facilitate your search, and certain kinds of sweatsuits are both warm and stretchy. Watch out for sweat pants that are baggy below the knee, however. You could easily snag the toe pick or the heel of the blade on them, causing an unnecessary and unpleasant fall.
- As your skating expertise increases, you'll want to start wearing clothing that shows off your body line—in other words, you'll want it to be tight. Body line and position are very important in skating, and you want your coach, choreographer, and admirers to be able to see your line and positions clearly. For a woman, a spandex outfit or a leotard and tights are suitable for practice. In competition, women are now required to wear a skirt. For a man, a tight-fitting sweatsuit or a speed-skating outfit is acceptable. Scott Hamilton wore a plain speed-skating-type outfit for

Competitive skaters wear clothing that shows off their body line.

his 1984 Olympic gold medal performance. It was sleek and form fitting; it showed his body line and yet allowed complete freedom of movement.

What this all boils down to is this: Be warm and comfortable, and yet give others the chance to enjoy your elegant line and your perfect positions.

Accessories

As you might expect, skating requires other pieces of equipment. Items such as scribes for practicing school figures, costumes, tapes, rule books, and magazine subscriptions will be required at various stages in your development as a skater. Since circumstances can arise suddenly in which you will need these items, it is best to be prepared in advance. These are some possible situations:

- Should you find yourself performing an exhibition in a local skating club show, you'll need a costume. If you intend to use the costume again, buying it or having it made (the latter being the more common case) can be justified. On the other hand, if it is a one-time event, renting the costume is the sensible alternative. When renting, you face the problem of finding an outfit that fits perfectly, but it's worth a try.

A scribe is a compass used to draw circles on the ice. Skaters follow the scribed imprint of a figure eight during warmups for compulsory figures.

- As your skating expertise improves, you will want to begin skating to music. This, of course, is an integral aspect of singles and pairs free skating, and of ice dancing, and constitutes a distinguishing feature of skating as compared to nearly all other sports. When you compete or skate an exhibition, music is a prerequisite to participation.
- A scribe is a compass that is used to draw circles on the ice. This is useful when practicing compulsory figures, the discipline that encompasses the proverbial figure eight. The scribe is used both for checking figures that have already been laid out on the ice and for inscribing a circle on the ice which the skater then follows. Both applications are used only in training and are not allowed in competitions.
- In any hobby, occupation, or sport, keeping abreast of ongoing developments is essential. Rule books and magazine subscriptions are a must as a source of information about current rules and regulations, and the trends that are prominent in the sport. A list of reading materials available is included in *The Skater's Handbook.*

GETTING STARTED

Once you have the equipment, the next step is to get the skates on your feet, *properly.* If you have purchased new boots, it is essential that you tie them correctly. If you don't, the process of breaking them in can ruin both the boots and your feet—the latter having consequences well beyond a skating career.

Lace 'Em Up

To put your skates on correctly from the very beginning and to break the boot in properly, just follow these steps.

1. Loosen the laces, especially at the instep, and slide the skate onto your foot while pulling up the tongue.

2. Start tightening the skate by pulling the laces firmly from the toe up to the bend of your ankle.

3. Around the bend of the ankle, keep the lacing loose enough to accommodate the forward flex that occurs there when you bend your knee, but tight enough to provide support. Although the skate will certainly not feel entirely comfortable when you bend your knee, it should feel reasonably comfortable when your ankle and knee are straight.

4. At the outset, lace only one hook above the ankle, firmly, and tie the laces.

5. After at least five outings in the new skates, lace up another hook at the top.

6. Continue to add a hook every time your boots begin to feel comfortable with the existing lacing scheme. When you reach the top two hooks, leave them a little looser than the eyes around the bend of the ankle, to allow the ankle to bend forward freely when the knee bends.

If the boots are very stiff, it's helpful to put on a pair of wet socks, then lace the boots up to the first hook and wear them around the house. Doing this 5 to 10 times for 20 minutes each time will make the break-in process on the ice much less forbidding. If you have purchased boots and blades separately, make sure that the blades are attached to the boots before carrying out this little trick; to protect both your blades and your floors, wear guards on the blades.

In fact, any time you have your skates on and you are not on the ice, the guards should be on the blades. The fine sharpening of the blades, essential for good skating, is easily damaged by grit, dirt, and hard surfaces. As an extra precaution, rinse the guards out every couple of weeks to remove the grit that

Skates

Properly laced skates are critical for your comfort and skating success.

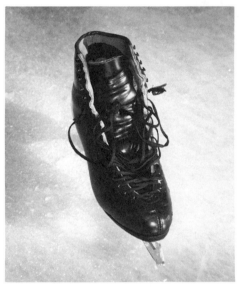

The deep creases in the tongue, and the shallow but visible creases in the side of the boot, indicate that this boot is broken in.

If the top flops to one side, the boot has broken down.

may have been trapped in them. Undamaged, properly sharpened blades make for a much happier and more promising practice session.

Boots are broken in when you can freely bend your ankle and knee. They are said to have broken down when the sides of the boot do not give the ankle any support, and the ankles simply flop from side to side. When this happens, you need new boots.

Once you have one foot firmly planted on the ice, hold the barrier with one hand and remove the guard from the other blade. Always wear skate guards when leaving the ice.

Onward to the Ice

Dressed and laced up, you are at the edge of the ice surface, ready to step onto the ice for your first glide. Before you do, let me caution you not to do what so many skaters, including myself, have done so many times—step on the ice with the guards still on the blades. This is not putting your best foot forward.

The first thing to do is to grasp the barrier with one hand and remove one guard from the blade with the other. Place the bare blade carefully on the ice; carefully because you want to give yourself the best opportunity to gain confidence. Then, keeping your weight on both feet, turn around so that you are facing the entrance, with your back to the rink. Pick up the foot that is still on Mother Earth and remove that guard; continue to hold on to the barrier while you do this. Place that foot down on the ice.

You now have both blades on the ice. Stand there a moment to gain your balance. While holding the barrier, slide the blades back and forth. This cools down the blades and gives you a sense of what it feels like to glide along the ice.

The next step is to turn around. Holding the barrier with one hand, turn yourself around so that your feet are parallel with the barrier. Place your feet about 12 inches apart, your weight evenly distributed between them, your knees slightly bent.

The next move is perhaps the most important you will ever make on the ice. Let go of the barrier. Just wait there, relax, and regain your balance before you embark on the first glide. From this point on, the principles and methods of skating are central to your progress.

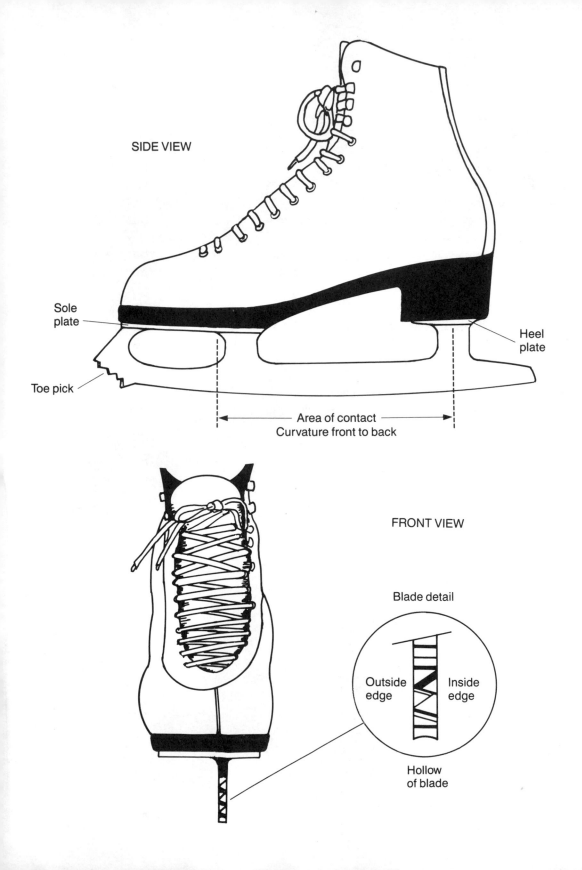

SIDE VIEW

Sole
plate

Heel
plate

Toe pick

Area of contact
Curvature front to back

FRONT VIEW

Blade detail

Outside
edge

Inside
edge

Hollow
of blade

2

Principles and Terminology

The physical principles that govern skating are far different from those that govern most other sports. The differences result from the nature of the medium and the nature of the equipment.

The medium, of course, is ice. As a skate blade moves across the ice, it produces friction. This friction creates heat, which melts the ice. In essence, skaters skate on a thin film of water.

The equipment also has unique properties. A skate blade has two edges running down its length. Between the two edges is a valley, or "hollow." A skater spends most of the time on only one of the edges, rather than on both simultaneously (skating on both edges is known as skating on the flat of the blade). It is as though you were standing on the edge of a knife. In addition, the blade is curved from end to end. This means that only a small portion of the blade is in contact with the ice at any one time.

These factors dictate that you will almost always be leaning to one side or the other, producing a curved line, or imprint, on the ice. And that means that unlike most sports, which are governed predominantly by linear motion, nearly all aspects of skating involve a multiplicity of linear and *rotational* forces which, combined, are known as angular momentum. Having to control all these forces, lest one of them causes you to fall, is the fundamental reason for the high level of precision required in skating.

According to physical principles, the primary force governing figure skating is *angular momentum.* Angular momentum is a combination of linear motion (motion in a straight line) and rotational motion (motion in a circle around a single point). Linear motion can occur on a horizontal plane, as in running on dry land, or in a vertical plane, as in jumping up and down in one place. Rotational motion can occur in two directions: clockwise or counter-

31

Anatomy of a figure-skating blade. To produce two edges along the length of the blade, a hollow is ground down its center.

clockwise. When linear and rotational motion are combined, the forces exerted on a skater's body become quite complex.

The combination of horizontal linear motion and rotation in one direction produces angular momentum as the skater glides across the ice. Remember that in order to skate on the edge of the blade, the skater's body is leaning to one side or the other. The degree of lean determines the curvature of the imprint on the ice, which, in turn, conveys rotational momentum to the skater's body. As you will learn, each type of edge possesses an inherent direction of rotation. For example, skating on the forward right outside edge inherently rotates the skater in the clockwise direction, while skating on the forward left outside edge inherently rotates the skater in the counterclockwise direction. When this inherent rotation is coupled with linear motion, and if it is left unchecked, it will make all parts of the body rotate in the same direction.

The skater faces further complexities when vertical linear motion is added to horizontal linear motion and rotational motion. This occurs on jumps. Since nearly all jumps involve a take-off from a particular edge, the path of the jump is on a curved line. The combination of these forces results in the skater becoming a trajectory that is governed by forces in three dimensions: horizontal linear, vertical linear, and rotational. In jumps, then, an exceedingly complex form of angular momentum governs the body.

The practical aspect of these physical principles becomes apparent in the context of particular elements. For example, to execute a spin, you must first harness the appropriate amount of rotational momentum from angular momentum. The entrance into the spin consists of both horizontal linear motion and rotational motion. Once in the spin, you are essentially dealing in one dimension—rotation around a single point. The transition from movements on a two-dimensional level to movements on one isn't easy. It requires you to convert the linear part of the angular momentum created for the entrance into virtually pure rotational momentum for the spin.

Jumps are even more difficult in that a third dimension pertains: vertical linear motion. This additional force creates a trajectory which is governed by the following:

1. the amount of upward force versus the force of the horizontal linear motion; and

2. the amount of rotational momentum created by the edge and the body movements.

These forces are produced by the speed across the ice, the degree of body lean, the speed and path of movement of the arms and free leg, the speed of

Motion and Angular Momentum in Figure Skating

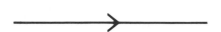

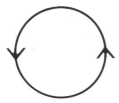

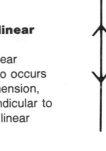

Horizontal linear motion.
Horizontal linear motion occurs in one dimension.

Vertical linear motion.
Vertical linear motion also occurs in one dimension, but perpendicular to horizontal linear motion.

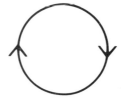

Rotational motion.
Rotational motion is in two dimensions, and is either counterclockwise (left) or clockwise (right).

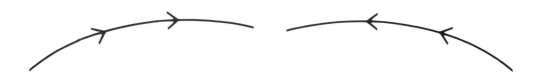

Angular momentum.
Angular momentum has an inherent rotational motion, either clockwise (left) or counter-clockwise (right).

Angular momentum.
Angular momentum occurs in three dimensions (as during jumps) and is a combination of horizontal and vertical linear motion and rotational motion.

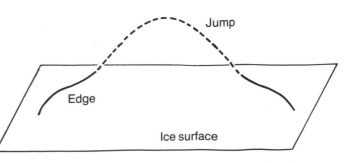

Jump

Edge

Ice surface

rotation of the body, and the strength of the spring from the ice. The need for precise control of all these movements and positions is one of the reasons that skating technique has not become standardized and that proficiency requires a fair amount of time and practice.

While these many forces make skating challenging and sometimes difficult, they also provide the foundation for our being able to execute on the ice many interesting and beautiful maneuvers that cannot be performed on dry land. As you'll see, the culprits of challenge and difficulty are the perpetrators of interest and beauty.

TERMINOLOGY

Modern figure skating was born during the last half of the nineteenth century. As a consequence of the sport's fairly lengthy history, a large body of terminology has evolved. Throughout this book, I use many terms that require special definition. For now, let's define the general terminology and conventions that the skater or serious skating enthusiast should know.

Edge

An edge is the side of the blade on which you are skating. The imprint that the edge of the blade makes on the ice is also called an edge. It is always curved and therefore is creating a circle. When you step on an edge, rotational momentum, lean, and linear momentum come together.

Flight Path

"Flight path" refers to the route you follow as you glide along the ice or jump into the air. This route can be reduced to a series of lines, which resemble a road map. "Line of flight" and "imprint" are synonymous with flight path.

Circle

One common flight path in skating is a circle. When you step onto an edge, you will begin to skate a circle. If you skate only a part of the circle before changing feet—say, one quarter—the concept of a circle with a single center point, and the lean required to skate the one quarter of that circle, still pertain. When a complete circle is not actually skated, I refer to the edge as an "imaginary circle."

Circle.
Every edge creates a circle. When less than an entire circle is skated, the part not skated is referred to as "imaginary."

Edge actually skated

Imaginary part of edge that completes the circle

A single edge can evolve from a large circle to a small one. Since the lean of the body and the speed over the ice determine the diameter (or radius) of the circle, an edge consisting of a constant degree of lean with a constantly declining speed produces a smaller and smaller circle as the edge proceeds. A circle with a single diameter and only one push at the beginning of the edge requires a decreasing lean as speed diminishes.

The lean required to create a circle is always toward the precise center of the circle—the spot where you would place the point of a compass when drawing a circle on a piece of paper.

Constant lean.
If the lean remains constant on a given edge, a gradual decrease in speed will result in a gradually decreasing circle size.

Degree

I often refer to a specific degree of lean or rotation. "Degree" refers to the angle produced by two objects. For example, a 70-degree lean means that the body is forming a 70-degree angle with the ice. Another example is a shoulder line which produces a 45-degree angle with the flight path or skating foot. This means that a line drawn from one shoulder to the other forms a 45-degree angle with the skating foot or the imprint on the ice. If the shoulders are perpendicular to the skating foot—that is, they are "square"—they will form a 90-degree angle.

Imprint

The imprint is the mark on the ice produced by the skate blade. It creates the road map and shows the flight path. It is particularly useful in analyzing technique, since the body motions create the force that dictates where the skating foot goes.

3

Body Positions

All too frequently, the subject of body positions is placed on a back burner until the skater "knows all the basics." Unfortunately, delays in attending to this aspect of skating more often than not allow the skater to develop bad habits. I have seen many fine skaters run into severe technical and artistic barriers at the peak of their careers because insufficient emphasis was placed on the subject early on. This is the last thing that a skater needs to worry about a few months before an Olympic trial!

Luckily for me, I learned about body position early in my career. As I have already suggested, at the outset I did not show a lot of promise as a skater. Body positions were irrelevant as far as I was concerned. In fact, my basic body positions were so primitive that fellow skaters likened me to a member of the simian species! Fortunately, a dramatic turnaround occurred early enough for me to transform that simian style into one that became rather classical. The catalyst for this change was my coach, Arthur Bourque, who taught me the importance of body positions. The moment of enlightenment took place just before I turned 14—none too soon.

If you're smart, you'll understand that basic body positions are critical to your progress as a skater and that now is the time to confront them. Since there are many variations in basic positions for each individual move, the discussion will describe only the fundamental positions for the different parts of the body.

THE BACK

This is where it all begins. The back is the main support for the rest of the body. It provides the pinion around which all the movements will occur, literally and

37

No skating technique can ever be successful without proper body position.

figuratively. If your back is weak or is ordinarily allowed to assume a weak position—that is, a slouch—you are setting yourself up for some severe problems that may be difficult to correct.

Quite simply, the back should be arched; not overly arched so that it looks swayed, like an old horse's, but properly arched, like a ballet dancer's. In fact, one way to learn how to arch the back is to take ballet lessons. Ballet dancers, perhaps more than any other artists or athletes, understand the importance of good body and back positions, and the significance of the back for overall balance and strength.

The concept of maintaining an arched back is not a difficult one, but few skaters, as it turns out, have good backs. Why? Because once they are on the ice, other considerations distract them from thinking about the back and can even cause them to choose an incorrect body position. For example, a slouched position makes it much easier to bend the knees to gain speed and to spring into a jump. It takes less strength and energy to accomplish the jump, although

The Back

Slouched shoulders and a drooping head constitute very poor skating posture (A).

On the other hand, a swayed back will prevent you from achieving rapid yet fluid movements and proper balance (B).

Standing erect is the most important basic position (C).

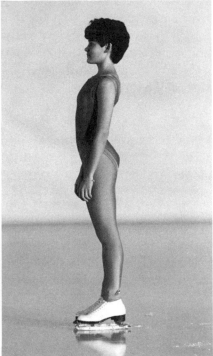
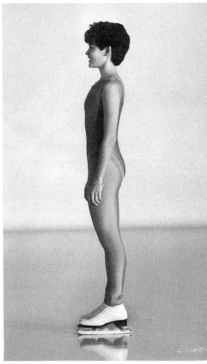

the skater inevitably falls short of the athletic and artistic goal. To increase speed and jump high with the back arched requires strength in the quadriceps (the upper thigh muscles in the front of the leg) and a substantial output of energy. Doing it right requires more of the skater at the outset. In the end, however, the skater gets more for the extra energy expended.

THE HEAD

Compared to the back, the head is relatively easy to control, but no less important. I can recall numerous examples of skaters failing to successfully execute critical jumps in the midst of their programs at World Championships because of lack of head control. Needless to say, this small fault prevented them from capturing the title.

Quite simply, the head should be held with the chin up. The ballet dancer is again a suitable model for the correct head position. One way to avoid a droopy head is to refrain from looking at the ice. Instead, look above the barrier or into the bleachers to keep your chin up. Also, while looking down will impair only your appearance on the ice when you are just skating around, it can seriously impair your ability to jump and spin, possibly even to the point that you can hardly land a jump.

Remember, proper head position is as easily learned as it is forgotten, and you should constantly remind yourself to look to the sky!

THE ARMS

Unlike the head and the back, arm positions vary according to the particular move being executed. While the movements of the arms will be described in detail for each move, four general points deserve attention.

First, the arms should be supported from the shoulders. In other words, the arms are not held out to the side as a result of straightening the elbow and wrist and tensing the forearm. The shoulders should bear the weight of the arms.

Second, when neither technique nor choreography requires specific arm movements, the arms should not droop in a meaningless fashion. Rather, they should be held out to the side in a relaxed fashion with only a slight downward angle, so that the hands are at a height which is just below the armpits.

Third, at no time should any tension be perceptible in any part of the shoulder, arm, wrist, or hand. A slight bend at the elbow, an even slighter bend at the wrist, and a soft curve to the hand and fingers will convey a sense of

The proper basic position of the arms, as shown here, is essential for balance and beauty.

relaxation. The shoulders, while relaxed, should appear to be the source of support and strength and should convey a sense of control.

Finally, arm movements should be fluid and lyrical unless the choreography or the technical requirements of the maneuver require something different. Peggy Fleming, the 1968 Olympic Gold Medalist, was known for her lyrical arm movements.

THE LEGS

The legs execute the technical maneuvers and the choreography, but are not merely servants to the various maneuvers; they do have a life of their own. For example, when you are gliding on one leg (the skating leg), the other leg (the "free leg") may be off the ice. It can be bent or straight, the foot turned in or out, the toe pointed down or up. Four general points are pertinent here:

First, when the skating leg has no other function, it should generally be bent slightly.

Second, unless otherwise indicated, the free leg should be straight, the foot turned out, and the toe pointed downward.

Third, the free leg should never be allowed to dangle. Unlike the arms, the knee of the free leg should be locked, the ankle tight, and tension should be visible in the pointed toe.

Finally, support and strength should originate from the hip and should be visible from the thigh down to the toe.

When you glide on one leg, the free leg should be straight, with the toe pointed and the leg supported at the hip.

4

First Strides and Glides

Not long ago, beginners used to skate first by walking, then by sculling. We now know that while walking can be helpful at the very outset, too great a dependence on this method only prolongs the learning process and delays the first experience of the gliding sensation. Happily, this out-of-date method has generally been replaced by starting immediately with sculling. So here we go!

SCULLING

Prior to our discussion about principles, terms, and body positions, you were standing on the ice next to the barrier, feeling, for the first time, what it is like to balance yourself on narrow blades without the benefit of grasping something immobile. It is now time to take your first solo step. Before you do, you will want to move a little farther away from the barrier. The rule of thumb is to keep a minimum distance of about 1½ times your height between you and the barrier, for three very good reasons. The most important reason has to do with safety. Should you fall, you won't hit your head or any other part of your body on the barrier. Such a collision could occur quite unexpectedly and could result in a serious injury. The nice thing about falling on the ice surface itself is that it is always flat, making it relatively easy to learn how to fall safely. Second, by staying some distance away from the barrier, your arms will be free to move as needed without encountering the obstruction of the barrier or the hockey glass. Finally, remaining out of reach of the barrier has a psychological benefit. When you remain close to the barrier, the temptation is to reach out and grasp it when you feel your balance deserting you. Instead, what you should be doing right from the beginning is trying to regain your balance without the crutch

43

Your first strides on ice need not be walking steps.
Glide!

of a support. This kind of struggle for balance represents the most efficient and expeditious way to learn where your balance is. Also, a barrier that is too close can stifle your sense of freedom, creating unnecessary tension.

To move out from the barrier: First, from your present position near the barrier with your feet 12 inches apart, pick up the foot nearest the barrier and place it right next to the other foot. Next, take the foot farthest from the barrier and move it away, so that the feet are again at least 12 inches apart. Repeat this sidestep until you are 1½ body lengths away from the barrier. (This kind of sidestepping movement is used to measure circles in the compulsory figures, when you want to ascertain that the lobes of the figure eight all have the same dimensions. So you need not feel shy about sidestepping; expert skaters do it all the time!)

Your final sidestep should position your feet about six inches apart, with your weight evenly distributed between them. Hold your arms straight out from your sides. Make certain that your chin is up and that you are looking straight ahead. Also be sure that your back is arched, and stand erect. If your ankles are straight and not flopped to one side, you are now on your first edge. It just so happens that both feet are on inside edges. The angle of the legs from the hips, created by the position of your feet, will automatically place you on the inside edge of the blade. You are now ready to scull forward:

1. Bend your knees.
2. Turn your toes out slightly, away from each other.
3. Let your skates glide in the direction indicated by your toes. You can help start the glide by bending your knees a little more and exerting a little pressure against the ice.
4. As the feet start to move out from under you, begin straightening your knees and turn your toes in, as though you were slightly pigeon-toed. As you do this, start pulling your feet back together again. If you forget to pull your feet together, you will end up in a perilous position with your legs apart and at a dead stop. If this should happen, your only option is to collapse to the ice and start again.

Once your feet are moving toward each other, you are on your way back to the original position. Since you will start the motion again without stopping, allow your feet to come within about six inches of each other before repeating the sculling motion. The idea is to scull continuously. It may sound boring, but it is an important exercise that enables you to gain confidence on two feet before embarking on one.

Although sculling sounds simple enough, you may encounter some difficulty in picking up speed. Of all the aspects of sculling, this happens to be the most challenging at the outset. Bending and straightening the knees at the appropriate times is what creates speed: bending as your toes move out, straightening as they move in. The coordination of these movements requires a good sense of timing, and you might want to enlist a teacher or friend to help you with them. Have him or her gently push you forward. Since speed no longer represents a problem, you have only to think about the coordination of your knee bend with your feet positions to achieve the snakelike motion.

A good way to practice forward sculling is to go back and forth across the end of the rink. That way, you can use the barrier to help you turn yourself around for the return journey. Also, you will be out of the way of the more aggressive skaters, who normally use the center part of the ice surface.

When you feel competent sculling forward, it's time to entertain the thought of going backward. Once entertained, it's time to act!

As you did with forward sculling, get in position with your feet six inches apart, arms out, back arched, and head up. Backward sculling is virtually the same as forward sculling, except that the starting position of the feet is different. Your feet will start pointing in toward each other, and will end up pointing away from each other.

1. Bend your knees.
2. Turn your toes in toward each other, slightly pigeon-toed.
3. Push against the ice to start the glide.
4. Once you are on the move and your feet are 12 to 18 inches apart, straighten your knees slowly, turn your feet out so that the toes point away from each other, and pull your feet back together.
5. When you arrive back at the starting position, repeat the entire motion without stopping.

As you become proficient at sculling, you can start doing it faster, and you can make the expanding and contracting movement more exaggerated by letting your feet move farther apart and bringing them closer together on each scull. Good sculling habits lead to good inside edges—an integral ingredient of your next move.

Sculling

In the set-up position for forward sculling, shown here, the feet are about six inches apart, the weight is evenly distributed between both feet, the legs are straight, the arms are in the basic position, and the body is erect (A).

To initiate the sculling motion, bend your knees (B).

Allow your feet to move away from each other and your legs to straighten once you begin to glide (C).

To return to the starting position, begin to point your toes in (D).

Pull your feet together until the toes are nearly touching (E), then repeat the action.

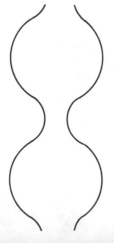

Sculling produces a symmetrical, snake-like imprint on the ice.

5

Stroking and Crossovers

Thus far, your experience on the ice has been virtually riskless. Both feet have been on the surface to support you, making the ice seem almost like dry land. Now that you have your sculling down, it's time to begin skating on one foot. As it turns out, it is almost easier to stand on one foot on the ice than it is to stand on one foot on the ground. When you first try it, you probably won't believe me. However, given some time and a little speed, you will begin to understand how easy it really is.

STROKING

The easiest way to achieve facility in skating on one foot is to begin with stroking. This is essentially the process of pushing with one foot, then the other, to gain speed.

When you stroke, you use the two edges of the blade: the outside edge and the inside edge. Remember, edges run down the length of the blade and are created by a U-shaped hollow in the blade. When blades are sharpened, not only are the edges made sharper, but the hollow is also restored. The inside edges are the ones on the inside of your foot. The outside edges are the ones on the outside of your foot. When you skate on both edges simultaneously, you are skating on the flat of the blade.

Not surprisingly, there are two levels of stroking: one for the beginner and one for the more advanced skater. The beginner's stroking method consists of short strokes. The more advanced version requires long edges and elaborate transitions between positions.

49

As Tracie Brown demonstrates here, stroking and gliding forward on one skate is a fundamental figure-skating maneuver.

Beginner's Stroking: Forward

The first step, familiar to you by now, is to place yourself on the ice away from the barrier. Stand erect, head up. Proper posture will help you avoid the feared calamity: hitting the toe pick, which creates a forward fall. Face the direction in which you intend to skate. This part of the setup is somewhat like that used for sculling, and will be employed many times for a variety of skating moves.

The Setup:

1. With your feet together, make certain that you have your balance.
2. Hold your arms out at your sides.
3. Arrange your feet in a "T" formation, the right foot (the foot that will become the skating foot) pointing in the direction in which you intend to skate and the left foot perpendicular to, and behind, the right foot. The heel of the right foot should be touching the instep of the left foot. You should be standing on the flats of the blades.
4. In setting up your feet, your shoulders may have turned counterclockwise slightly. To offset this, place your left arm slightly in front of you, while keeping your right arm out to the side, parallel to the left foot.

You now have completed the setup. In preparation for the push-off, bend both knees. As you bend, you will be tempted to lunge forward. Try to avoid this by concentrating on standing erect. Your coach may help you by placing a cup of coffee on your head, with the stipulation that spilled coffee means a lesson that costs twice as much. Keep your back straight.

Forward Stroking and Gliding

To begin, the feet should form a "T" in preparation for the push-off onto a forward edge (A). Hold your left arm in front of you, your right arm to the side (B). Bend the knees for the push-off (C). After the push-off, extend the free leg and keep the skating knee bent (D). As you approach the point of transition from one foot to the other, straighten the skating leg and begin to change the position of the arms (E). As you shift your weight to your left foot and push off onto it, extend your right arm in front and your left arm to the side (F).

A

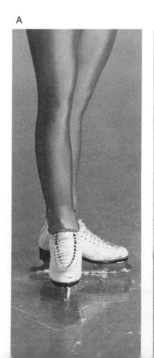

B

C

1. To begin moving, push the left foot against the ice, allowing the right foot to glide forward. In a perfect push, only the inside edge of the pushing foot makes contact with the ice, and the left toe pick does not leave a mark on the ice. To do this, concentrate on pushing with the instep of the left foot. As the left foot leaves the ice, point the toe.

2. As you push, transfer your weight almost entirely to your right foot. The weight will be on the flat of the blade as the push-off is executed and will automatically shift to a gentle inside edge as the left foot is released from the ice.

3. The thrusting movement consists of straightening the left leg as the push-off is executed. The right leg should remain bent to cushion the transfer of weight.

4. During the push-off, the left arm and shoulder will tend to move back. To prevent this, extend the left arm slightly to keep it in front.

Once the weight has been fully transferred to the right foot and the left foot is off the ice, the push-off is complete. Bring the left foot alongside the right foot as smoothly as possible. (Jerking it can cause you to lose your balance.) This is the moment when you will make most progress toward gaining a sense of balance on the ice. The slower you execute this movement, the more time you will spend on one foot. The more time you spend on one foot, the faster you will acquire a solid sense of balance. The objective during practice sessions is gradually to increase the length of time you take for this movement.

D

E

F

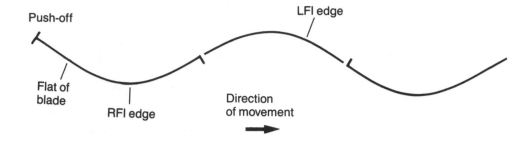

Push-off

LFl edge

Flat of
blade

RFl edge

Direction
of movement

Pattern of the imprint on the ice produced by basic forward stroking.

Bringing your feet together should be coordinated with a change in your arm positions, the left moving to the side and the right to a position slightly in front. It is now time to try stroking on the other foot.

The Transition:

1. Place your left foot on the ice parallel and next to your right foot. Distribute your weight evenly between the two feet, on the flats of the blades.

2. Bend your knees again.

3. Since you now have a little speed over the ice, this push-off will be slightly different from the first. The thrust will still be from the inside edge of the blade, with no toe-pick involvement. Push against the ice with your right foot. Turn your right toe out slightly and allow the right foot to move to the side and behind as you push. If you don't turn your foot out as you push, the toe pick will inevitably dig into the ice.

4. As you push, shift your weight to your left foot. The shift in weight will cause your right foot to move away from you and your right leg to straighten. As your weight shifts, the left foot will change from the flat of the blade to the inside edge. As you lift your right foot off the ice, don't forget to point your toe!

From here on in, the action is the same as it was for the left foot: The right leg is lifted off the ice and brought smoothly alongside the left foot as the arms change position, and you shift to the right foot. This stroking procedure can be followed as you skate around the rink, or, if you find yourself on a frozen canal in Holland, to skate the "Elfstedentocht," an 11-city, 199-kilometer race that starts and finishes in Leeuwarden.

Beginner's stroking will take you down the side of the rink without problems, but the corners will be difficult to negotiate without the help of crossovers, which we will describe shortly. For the time being, the beginner should try either to negotiate the corners while stroking or simply glide on two feet around the corners.

Beginner's Stroking: Backward

Stroking backward poses more difficulties for the beginner, for two reasons. First, you are not able to see where you are going. Second, the physical principles are somewhat unnatural, since our feet point forward, not backward, and our knees bend in only one direction, forward. The body positions and movements make the more advanced level of backward stroking, which is primarily composed of backward crossovers, markedly easier. But first you must learn the seemingly more difficult beginner's method since this requires fewer movements, less speed, and a less refined sense of balance.

As you did in forward stroking, place yourself 1½ body lengths away from the barrier before you begin the setup.

The Setup:

1. Stand erect, with your head up and your arms out to the side.
2. Place your weight evenly between your feet, which should be about six inches apart. You will be standing virtually on the flats of the blades.
3. Bend your knees.

The Push-Off:

1. While keeping your right foot parallel to your intended line of flight, turn the left in so that your left toe is pointing generally in the direction of the right foot—a half-pigeon-toed position.
2. To execute the push-off, press against the ice with your left foot as you straighten your left knee. You will begin to move backward, away from the starting point.
3. As you begin to move, pull your left leg back ever so slightly. This will result in a back inside edge push-off that, while short, has a slight curve. In this push-off, the toe pick will graze the ice. Minimizing toe-pick involvement is the goal; eliminating it is both impossible and undesirable since it helps stabilize

the foot on the ice and therefore increases the force of the push-off.

4. As the push-off is taking place, shift your weight to your right foot, and gradually change from the flat of the blade to the inside edge. Since some of the body's weight remains on the left foot during the push-off, the change of edge should occur more or less automatically. Be sure that your weight is about on the center of the blade (the instep).

Let your left foot drag on the ice following the push-off. Once you feel comfortable skating backward, you can pick up your left foot. It will be positioned slightly in front of you and to the side. Again, the longer you remain on one foot, the faster you will acquire a sense of balance.

When you have had enough of this one-foot business, or when your speed is decreasing to the extent that it is threatening your balance, place your left foot on the ice parallel to and about six inches away from the right foot. You will again be on the flats of the blades, ready for the next push-off.

Since you now are gliding across the ice, some minor adjustments must be made in the manner in which you execute the next push-off.

The Transition:

1. Bend your knees, remembering to maintain an erect posture.

2. Push against the ice with your right foot, turning the foot in a pigeon-toed position. The degree of the pigeon-toe will be less severe than when executing the push-off from a standstill. When pushing off from a standstill, the thrusting foot is nearly perpendicular to the path of flight, an impediment to forward motion. An important first principle of skating is that blades move only forward and backward across the ice—not laterally, except under force.

3. Simultaneously shift your weight to the inside edge of your left foot. Be certain that the weight is on the instep, or middle, of the left foot.

4. Once the feet are about 18 to 30 inches apart, either pick up the right foot or let it glide along the ice.

5. Continue the process, placing the right foot parallel to the left, and then pushing off with the left.

Throughout this movement, you must maintain an erect body position, with your head up. At this early stage it is also very important to concentrate on keeping your arms out to the side in a relaxed fashion. Rigidity is always to be avoided. During the actual push-offs some torso movement is natural, but should only be slight.

The decision concerning whether or not to lift the thrusting foot off the ice depends on your level of confidence. However, you must not postpone it for too long, since this will lead to an unnecessary dependence on two-foot skating.

D

Backward Stroking and Gliding

The set-up position for basic backward stroking is virtually the same as that for sculling (A). Bend the knees and pigeon the toes in (B). As you push with the left foot, shift your weight to the right (C). If you are comfortable with your balance, lift your left foot (D).

C

Pattern of the imprint on the ice produced by backward stroking using the beginner's technique.

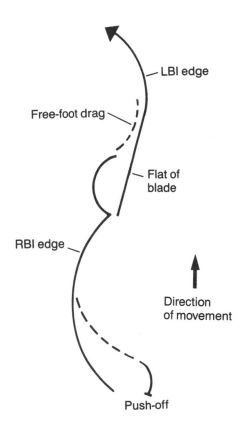

LBI edge

Free-foot drag

Flat of blade

RBI edge

Direction of movement

Push-off

B

A

CROSSOVERS

You will quickly discover that although stroking enables you to skate comfortably in a straight line, negotiating the corners presents some problems. Crossovers are the solution to this difficulty. Without a doubt, crossovers are the staple of every skater. Not only are they used to negotiate corners, but they are also used to pick up speed. When an advanced skater performs a free-skating program in a World Championships, for example, crossovers invariably comprise the primary link between jumps, spins, and footwork sequences. In an original free-skating program, the skater traverses about 600 meters. Crossovers enable the skater to cover this distance in less than three minutes. Skating without crossovers would be virtually unthinkable.

Since crossovers are used to negotiate corners, it's not surprising that the best way to learn them is on a circle. In some rinks, hockey circles are painted in the corners or the center of the ice and can serve as paths to follow. One word of caution before you begin: Be careful that you don't concentrate so much on the circle that you drop your chin and end up looking at the ice.

Forward Crossovers

Once you have chosen your place on the ice—away from the barrier, of course—stand with your feet together. Assume an erect position. The proper setup is critical to the easy execution of crossovers and constitutes your first alteration of the fundamental frontal torso position.

The Setup:

With your arms dangling at your sides, turn your shoulders counterclockwise so that your left shoulder is back and your right is in front. Ideally a line drawn between your shoulders should be effectively parallel to your line of flight. You should establish this position using only the back muscles: your arms should be completely relaxed. If you can move your arms freely while maintaining your torso position, you have employed the correct muscles to get into position.

Correctly assuming the setup position is important for two reasons. First, the arms are now free to carry out artistic movements without influencing balance or position. Second, assuming the correct shoulder position (using the back and not the arms) prevents the trailing shoulder from rolling forward. A rolled shoulder produces a weak position and an ugly line. Regrettably, the majority of skaters, beginners and experts, suffer from this problem. This is a clue to the intensity of concentration required to achieve the correct body position for crossovers.

1. Raise your arms to a relaxed skating position, right arm in front and left arm back.

2. While maintaining an erect torso, bend your knees.

3. Look forward in the direction of flight, and disregard the tendency to look into the center of the circle around which you are skating.

The Push-Off:

The setup has now placed you into a position to execute forward crossovers in a counterclockwise direction.

1. Push against the ice with the right foot. The direction of the force should be to the side and back.

2. Your diligence in practicing beginning forward stroking without toe-pick involvement will now pay off. Push from a forward inside edge, letting the right foot follow through out to the side.

3. As you push, shift your weight to your left foot, which is now on an outside edge. Initially, your body will lean only slightly into the circle.

4. Once your right foot leaves the ice at the end of the push, point your toe and straighten your right leg. Once secure, cross your right foot in front of the left. Place it on the ice with the outside of the right heel next to the little toe of the left foot. Keep your skating knee bent during the crossover motion.

Since the crossover motion is a relatively easy movement to execute, skaters frequently pay too little attention to it. However, two aspects of the motion are worth further discussion. First, the actual crossover motion will be different, depending on your level of expertise. The beginner will more than likely pick the foot up fairly high during the crossover motion. For the expert, however, the goal is to execute the crossover as close to the ice as possible, enhancing the appearance of a smooth, graceful movement. In addition, the positioning of the right foot as it crosses over the left and is placed on the ice is less well-defined in an expert's crossover. Second, the skating leg should always be bent. When both feet are on the ice during the push-off, both legs should be bent. A skater should never bounce up and down while executing crossovers.

D

C

E

B   A

To establish a shoulder line parallel to the feet for forward crossovers, use your back muscles, keeping your arms and shoulders relaxed (A). Once the shoulders are properly positioned, raise the arms and bend the knees (B). Push off with the right foot, moving it back and to the side while shifting your weight to the left leg (C). Extend your free foot to the side, keep your skating leg bent, and lean into the circle (D). Cross the right foot over the left and push out to the side with the left foot (E). Bring the right foot next to the left to repeat the process.

The Transition:

1. Next, start to shift your weight to the inside edge of the right foot.

2. As you shift your weight, your left foot should push against the ice and glide on an outside edge behind your right foot—out to the side, that is, outside the circle. (The beginner will find it difficult pushing from the left foot and will generally shortchange the power of the push. For the expert, constant practice aimed at improving the power of this stroke is essential. One exercise is to stand

with your weight predominantly on your right foot, in the crossover position, and with the right leg bent. From this position, repeatedly push with the left foot, keeping it behind and to the side of the right foot.)

    3. Once you complete the push, your right foot should be carrying all the weight.

    4. Pick up the left leg, uncross it, and place it directly next to the right foot inside the circle.

    5. Repeat.

As you achieve more and more facility with the technique, keep a number of key points in mind. First, it is absolutely essential to maintain the setup torso position. Second, the knee bend should remain constant as you execute the crossover. Another way to think about this is to maintain a constant distance between the top of your head and the ice. This serves both to conserve energy and to maximize the power of the push. Third, you achieve maximum power when your feet are next to each other at the beginning of the thrust and half your weight is on the thrusting foot. Increased weight on the thrusting foot and a thrusting position close to the center of the push increase the potential for power. As the thrusting foot moves farther away from the skating foot, the power that it can produce declines dramatically. Fourth, the push-off should resemble an explosion. You should strive to execute a thrusting motion as fast as possible. This not only will produce maximum power, but it will also build the muscles required for jumping and landing.

    By simply reversing the direction, you can perform crossovers on a circle going in the clockwise direction.

Backward Crossovers

The setup for backward crossovers is virtually the same as the setup for forward crossovers, and equally important. Assume the same torso position, with your chest facing the inside of the circle around which you will be skating, this time in a clockwise direction. Turn your head to look inside the circle and back. Lift your arms so that your left arm is back and your right arm is in front. Your feet should be together.

The Push-Off:

    1. Bend your knees.

    2. Lift your left foot, placing it on an outside edge about 12 inches away

from your right foot and toward the inside of the circle. You will be leaning slightly to the center of the circle. This lean should never be too severe, since keeping your weight directly over the foot carrying most of it will accomplish three goals: First, it will help you keep your back straight; second, it will help you maintain your balance; and third, it will provide the optimal conditions for maximum power on the thrust.

3. Push against the ice with your right foot, allowing it to turn in to a slightly pigeon-toed position. The right foot will execute the thrust from an inside edge. As you push, the right foot will move away from the left foot, and you will begin gradually to shift all of your weight to the left foot. Remember, as more weight is shifted to the left foot, thrusting power declines. Thus, most of the power from the stroke comes at the beginning of the push-off.

The Transition:

1. Once the push-off is complete, pick up the right foot and cross it over in front of the left foot, placing it on the ice next to the outside of the left foot. If you are an advanced skater, you will virtually drag the right foot across. The objective is to execute this motion in as fluid a manner as possible. This can be most easily accomplished when the crossover motion of the right foot is done close to the ice.

2. Shift the weight to the inside edge of the right foot and put some pressure on the left as the weight is shifted. The power generated by the left foot's thrust will be minimal, but important nonetheless.

3. Lift up the left foot. Keep it as close to the ice as possible, and step toward the inside of the circle.

4. Repeat the motion, beginning with the push-off described above for the standing start.

These instructions apply to crossovers in the clockwise direction. Like forward crossovers, back crossovers can also be executed moving counterclockwise. In fact, a skater should strive to achieve equally strong forward and backward crossovers in both directions. As we'll see later, practicing crossovers in both directions will benefit your efforts on jumps and spins.

The manner in which back crossovers are executed will vary dramatically from level to level. As a beginner, your movements will be segregated as you work to master the movements. The goal, however, is to achieve fluidity, and as you become more proficient, the motion will become much smoother. For example, as the leg away from the center of the circle is crossing over, the inside

Back Crossovers

A   B   C

Set up for a clockwise back crossover the same way you did for counterclockwise forward crossovers. In this case, however, look back over your left shoulder (A). Bend your knees and push off with your right foot (B). After you have shifted your weight to the left foot (C), begin to cross the right foot over the left. Shift your weight to your right foot as the crossover occurs, and push to the side with your left foot (D). As you lift your left leg at the end of the push-off, point your toe (E). Bring the free leg to the inside of the circle to prepare for the next push-off and the next wide step (F).

D

E

F

leg should already be moving behind and out of the circle. Similarly, as the outside leg begins to push against the ice, the inside leg should be moving into the circle for the step. This scissorlike motion should be continuous and grace-ful—which comes only with a great deal of practice and is most apparent at the Olympic level. In my opinion, the Russian pairs teams rank among the best when it comes to back crossovers. Russian skaters are known for their tremen-dous speed across the ice, which is a manifestation of their expertise with back crossovers.

Back crossovers represent the primary method for moving backward in figure skating and are the single best method for picking up speed. The power available from back crossovers is tremendous, provided that the skater main-tains a constant distance between his or her head and the ice surface, the knees are bent to the maximum, and the thrust is explosive.

Once you have become an expert at back crossovers, you can use this method of stroking for building strength and stamina. Alternating long periods of back crossovers—say four to five minutes—and short bursts, or a stop-start routine, can provide one of the best methods of on-ice training for stamina, speed, and agility.

ADVANCED FORWARD STROKING

Advance forward stroking is different from beginner forward stroking in only two respects. First, a greater amount of time is spent on one foot, and second, forward crossovers are an integral part of the exercise, which therefore will take up the entire ice surface. Of course, a certain increase in fluidity will also accompany the transition to the more advanced form of stroking.

Since you will use the entire ice surface, you will have some freedom in choosing the starting point. However, you will find it slightly easier if you begin near the middle of the rink, about 15 feet from the side barrier. By the time you reach the end of the rink, you will have picked up some speed for the crossovers.

You can, and should, skate around the rink in both directions; here I shall describe stroking in the counterclockwise direction.

In preparation for the push-off, bend your knees as much as possible while keeping your back arched. Push off with your left foot, allowing it to move to the side and back. Each push should carry you a substantial distance. You will alternate feet two more times, as described in the beginner stroking section. By this time, you should be approaching the end of the rink and standing on your right foot.

Bring your left arm back and your right arm forward. Your shoulders should initiate this movement in the same way that you set up for forward crossovers. Your torso should face toward the center of the rink.

As you change your arm and shoulder positions, bring your left foot alongside your right foot. Place your left foot on the ice next to your right foot. Begin forward crossovers around the end of the rink. When you reach the other side, push with your right foot, shifting your weight onto your left foot to begin stroking down the side.

You will now be skating at a fair pace. Each stroke down the side of the rink should result in your spending more time on each foot. Ideally, you should be able to propel yourself from one end of the rink to the other in only two strokes: the right foot push-off coming out of the crossovers and one more push-off coming from the left foot.

Your strokes down the side of the rink should be very smooth. Once you push off on a stroke, the motion should proceed slowly. None of the following movements should be completed until a split second before the next push-off.

- Gradually straighten the skating leg.
- Change the arm and shoulder positions gradually.
- Initiate the movement of the free leg to the skating leg slightly after the arm and shoulder movements begin. The free knee should be locked, with the toe pointed.
- At the beginning of the stroke, remain on the flat of the blade, shifting to a gentle inside edge about two thirds of the way through the stroke as your free leg approaches your skating leg.

Once these motions are completed, bend your knees and push with the other leg. Repeat the motion. Once at the end of the rink, begin crossovers as before.

ADVANCED BACKWARD STROKING

For the advanced skater, the best way to skate backward is to use back crossovers. While other forms of backward stroking exist, by and large they consist of connecting steps that are not employed for picking up speed but are used instead to link the different parts and maneuvers of a free-skating program.

6

Push-Offs and Edges

By now, you have had extensive informal experience skating edges during your stroking and crossover practices. In this section we will look at more formalized and disciplined methods of performing edges. Remember, proficiency on edges is one hallmark of a good skater.

Edges are the very foundation of skating. Nearly every important maneuver on the ice is done on them. If you can carry an edge well (that is, if you can skate for any distance on one edge or another), you have the basis for all other maneuvers. In addition, strong edges (being able to skate strongly on an edge) are indicative of good balance. Without a sense of balance, you will not be able to execute edges properly. Practicing edges in combination with stroking and crossovers is the best way to progress during the early stages of your skating career.

You will find that it is easiest to practice edges across the width of the ice surface. It is helpful at the outset if you can skate edges around a hockey line that extends from one side of the rink to the other. You will skate a semicircle on each foot, each semicircle starting and finishing at the line.

FORWARD OUTSIDE EDGES

The outside edge is the one that faces away from the opposite foot when the feet are together. Forward outside edges, or for that matter any edge, can be divided into four stages: the setup, the push-off, the execution, and the transition.

The Setup:

1. Place yourself on the ice, at least two body lengths from the barrier and facing the opposite side of the rink.

67

Proper edges require good balance and correct body position.

68

2. Turn one quarter revolution, so that you are facing the far end of the rink.

3. Form a "T" with your feet, your right toe pointing toward the far end of the rink and your left pointing toward the near side of the rink. Distribute your weight equally between your two feet and stand on the flats of the blades.

4. Place your right arm and shoulder in front and your left arm and shoulder back, so that the shoulders and arms form a line that is more or less parallel with the right foot.

5. Your torso will almost be facing the near side of the rink. You should be looking in the direction in which your right (soon to be skating) foot is pointing. A rule of thumb during forward edges: Always look in the direction you are skating. Keep your chin up.

The Push-Off:

1. Bend your knees.

2. Push against the ice with the inside edge of the left foot, making certain that the toe pick does not touch the ice. Shift your weight to your right foot as you push off.

3. Keep your hips tucked under your trunk as you push, and in a position that is perpendicular to the line of flight. When you push, you will be tempted to let your left hip slip back and your backside to stick out. Try to avoid these positions at all costs.

4. As you push, lean toward the skating, or right, shoulder—that is, into the center of the semicircle. A single, unbroken line should be formed by the body from the right shoulder down to the right foot. In other words, don't bend at the waist to create lean. By keeping the back arched, you can reduce the chance of bending at the waist.

The execution phase of any edge is perhaps the simplest technically, but the one that requires the most sophisticated sense of timing. It represents the first time that you will confront a credible amount of angular momentum (rotational plus linear motion). Controlling angular momentum, and utilizing it to the skater's benefit, requires some exquisite timing.

The Execution:

1. Raise your left foot behind you so that the instep of the free foot is approximately in line with the skating foot. The free leg should be bent slightly.

2. Gradually pass the left foot from behind to the front. The free foot should pass close by the skating foot as it comes in front, the hips remaining

more or less perpendicular to the line of flight. It is helpful to place moderate pressure on the left toe as it makes its pass and essential to point the toe once it is in front. The free foot should end up about six inches in front of the skating foot and slightly turned out. The passage of the free foot should occur smoothly, taking nearly as much time as it takes to skate the semicircle.

3. As the free leg moves in front, straighten it.

4. At the same time, move your arms around your body at a level that is no higher than the waist, the left coming in front and the right moving behind. This motion also should take place gradually over the entire semicircle. A common error is to allow the left shoulder and hip to drop as the rotation of the torso occurs. Keep your back arched and your lean constant (into the center of the semicircle) in order to prevent this mistake.

5. As the free leg, the arms, and the shoulders move to their new positions, lift over (that is, straighten) your skating leg. The straightening of your skating leg should proceed as gradually as did the free leg, arm, and shoulder movements.

6. During these movements, you should skate a complete half circle, returning to the line you are using as a reference; this line is called the long axis.

When you have arrived back at the long axis, it is time to switch feet and skate a semicircle on the left foot. At this point, you should be facing the other end of the rink, your left arm and shoulder in front, your right arm and shoulder behind.

1. Bring your left foot back so that it is alongside your right foot.

2. Place your left foot on the ice and bend your knees. For a split second, you will be skating on the flats of the blades.

3. Immediately turn your right foot out and push with the inside edge of the right foot onto the left outside edge. The left leg remains bent as the push-off is executed.

4. Repeat the movements described above, except in the opposite direction. The left arm and shoulder rotate to the back as the right arm and should come forward. The free leg and skating leg follow the same movements; the right leg is now the free leg, and the left is now the skating leg.

The smoother and more consistent the semicircle size and the degree of curvature, the more expert you will be deemed at doing edges. One important objective—which requires a great deal of practice—is the execution of "strong" edges, edges with a great deal of lean to the inside of the imaginary circle. Lean is what distinguishes beautiful skating from ordinary skating.

Forward Outside Edges

On the set-up for a right forward outside edge (shown here), hold your right arm and shoulder in front of you and your left arm and shoulder back (A). Your feet should be in the "T" position.

Bend your knees for the push-off (B).

Shift your weight to your right foot as you push with the left (C).

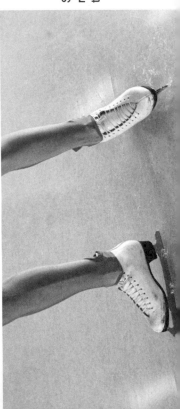

Pattern of the imprint on the ice produced by forward outside edges.

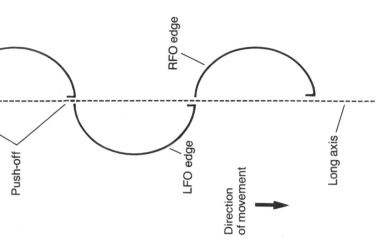

Short axis ----

Push-off

RFO edge

LFO edge

Direction of movement →

Long axis

After the push-off, let your left leg trail behind, slightly bent (D).

Rotate your arms and shoulders clockwise, and bring your free leg in front of you. As you execute this movement, straighten your skating leg (E).

At the long axis (see diagram), push onto your left foot (F).

FORWARD INSIDE EDGES

Inside edges involve skating on the inside edge of the blade, the edge of the blade facing the other foot. The same principles and objectives that applied to forward outside edges also apply to forward inside edges. Only certain specifics pertaining to the setup and the lean are different.

The Setup

1. Place yourself about two body lengths away from the barrier.
2. Face the far side of the rink.
3. Rotate one quarter turn clockwise, so that you end up facing the far end of the rink.
4. Form a "T" with your feet, the right foot pointing toward the far end of the rink and the left foot, perpendicular to the right, pointing toward the opposite side of the rink.
5. Make certain that your weight is equally distributed between your two feet and on the flats of the blades.
6. Place your left arm forward, parallel to the right foot, and your right arm to the side, parallel to the left foot.
7. Look in the direction in which you will be skating.

Now you are ready to push off. The push-off is exactly the same in principle as the push-off for the forward outside edge. Only two major differences apply: 1) you lean toward the free, or left, shoulder as you push off, in order to lean into the center of the semicircle, and 2) you push onto an inside edge as you shift your weight to the right foot. The execution is also the same, except that the passage of the free foot from the back to the front occurs on the inside of the circle and feels quite different. The rotational force during the edge can sometimes be stronger on inside edges than on outside edges, but it can be more easily controlled by pressing the free leg and hip forward after the free leg has passed in front. It is helpful to point the toe of the free foot.

Once you have returned to the long axis, real or imaginary, bring your left leg back toward the skating foot, and prepare to push off. Your right arm will be in front, your left arm back.

Pattern of the imprint on the ice produced by forward inside edges.

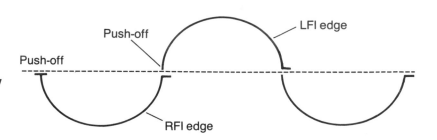

Push-off

Push-off

LFI edge

RFI edge

Direction of movement →

Forward Inside Edges

For a set-up for a right forward inside edge (shown here), position your left arm and shoulder in front of you, your right arm and shoulder back and to the side, and your feet in the "T" position (A). As you push with your left foot, shift your weight to your right leg and bend it (B). Rotate your arms and shoulders counterclockwise, move the trailing leg to the front, and gradually straighten your right knee (C). At the long axis (see diagram), switch foot positions and push with the right foot onto a left forward inside edge (D).

D

C

A

B

The Transition:

1. Place your left foot on the ice, temporarily distributing your weight equally between both feet and on the flats of the blades.

2. Bend your knees.

3. Turn your right foot out in preparation for the thrust.

4. Simultaneously move your right arm forward slightly, to a position nearly perpendicular to the long axis.

5. Execute the push-off and repeat the process.

Throughout the inside edges, remember to: 1) keep your chin up, 2) always look in the direction you are skating, 3) keep your back arched, 4) lean into the circle, 5) avoid bending into the circle, 6) make the rotational movements continuous, and 7) try to make the transitions from one foot to the other as smooth as possible.

BACK OUTSIDE EDGES

With the single exception of back crossovers, back outside edges represent probably the most important method of skating backward. Nearly all jumps involve a landing on a back edge. Exits from spins are often done on back outside edges. Without a strong foundation in back outside edges, the skater is severely handicapped.

The procedure for learning back outside edges may seem difficult at first. However, with persistence they quickly become second nature. Like forward edges, back outside edges involve the setup, the push-off, the execution, and the transition.

The Setup:

1. Place yourself about two body lengths from the edge of the rink, and face the opposite side.

2. Space your feet 12 to 18 inches apart. Distribute your weight evenly between your two feet, on the inside edges of the blades.

3. Place your right arm out to the side and your left arm pointing toward the far side of the rink. Keep your hands about waist level.

4. Keep your torso facing the opposite side of the rink, and look in that direction.

You are now in position for the push-off. The push-off itself was briefly discussed in the descriptions of back crossovers and stroking. However, when it is analyzed, the movement seems somewhat complicated. Once it becomes second nature, you will wonder why. Nevertheless, before describing the details of the body movement during the push-off, it is worth spending a moment to analyze the physical dynamics of the thrust.

The imprint made by the back push-off is quite distinct from that made by the forward push-off. While the forward push-off leaves the imprint of a straight line on the ice, the back push-off produces a curved line, the radius of which is large at the beginning, smaller in the middle, and larger again as the push-off comes to an end. In other words, the edge at the beginning and the end of the push-off tends to approach a straight line. The maximum power is generated near the beginning of the push-off, when most of the body weight is on the thrusting foot. This means that as the edge begins to move more in a straight line at the end of the push-off, the thrusting foot is less and less useful for generating speed. Therefore, it behooves the skater to concentrate most of the pushing force at the beginning of the push-off.

The execution of a back push-off is relatively complex. The thrusting leg straightens, pushing directly against the ice. This part of the thrust will generate nearly all of the power and thus, as discussed earlier, requires an explosive action. Simultaneously, the skate will move backward across the ice. While you need not consciously pull the skate back, you must allow it to happen. Remember, however, that the farther away the skate is from the starting point, the greater the reach required for the shift of weight to the skating foot. This complex interaction between pushing against the ice and moving away from the center of the thrust constitutes the unique motion of the back thrust.

The Push-Off:

1. Bend your knees.
2. Rotate your arms and shoulders counterclockwise. Simultaneously raise your right foot, stretching it across and behind your left leg and shifting all your weight onto the left foot. This will produce a more or less twisted position. Make certain that the twist is not too severe.
3. As you push off onto your right foot, unravel the twisted position. Bring the right arm back into a position parallel to the line of flight. Bring the left arm in front of you.
4. Step onto the right leg, keeping it bent.
5. As you step, your right foot should be placed on the ice on an outside edge, perpendicular to the long axis, with the toe pointing toward the long axis.
6. Raise your left foot in front of your right, leaving it at a comfortable

Pattern of the imprint on the ice produced by back outside edges.

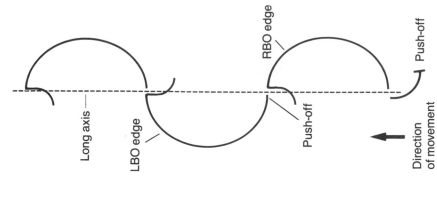

Long axis —

LBO edge

RBO edge

Push-off

Push-off

Direction of movement

Just before the long axis (see diagram), pull your left leg into the circle to enter the push-off (E), and execute the push-off onto your left back outside edge.

Rotate counter-clockwise to prepare for the transition (D).

After the push-off (C), your right arm and shoulder should be back, and your left arm, shoulder, and leg should be in front.

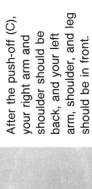

Look in the direction you will skate, and wind up for the push-off (B).

To set up for a right back outside edge, position your left arm in front and your right arm slightly back, and balance your weight equally on both feet (A).

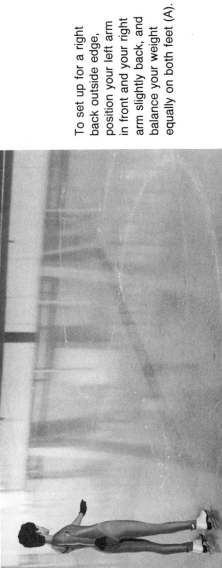

distance, about 12 inches, from the right foot. Turn the left foot out, point the toe, and straighten the left knee.

7. Lean toward the inside of the circle. It will feel as if you are leaning toward your right shoulder. Remember not to break at the waist to accomplish the lean.

The execution of a back outside edge involves many of the same principles that pertained to the forward edges. Fundamentally, the process is one of rotation.

The Execution:

1. Once on the back outside edge, begin the rotational motion: Rotate your arms and shoulders counterclockwise, the right coming in front and the left moving back, producing a shoulder line parallel to the skating foot.

2. At some point during the rotational motion, the head must also turn. For the beginner, the head can move continuously with the arms, shoulders, and torso. As you become more adept, you can postpone turning your head: For the first third of the edge, look to the inside and in the direction in which you are skating; then turn your head; this will take about another third of the edge; finally look outside and in the direction in which you are skating for the last third of the edge. The goal is to reduce the time required for the change of head position, minimizing the time during which you are unable to see where you are going.

3. As the edge progresses, pass your free leg back and straighten your skating leg. At the end of the movement, the free leg should be slightly bent and turned out, the instep of the free foot in line with the skating foot. Again, it is helpful to place some pressure on the toe as you pass it from front to back.

You should now be returning to the long axis, where you will switch feet. Although you now have some speed, you execute the push-off in the same way as you did from a standing position. The twist position is less severe in this case, as is the stretch of the free leg across and behind the skating leg. The rest of the push-off is the same as from a standing start.

The Transition:

1. As you approach the long axis, rotate the arms clockwise slightly, to create the twisted position.

2. Pull your free leg slightly back into the semicircle that has just been skated. This will draw you into the push-off.

3. Simultaneously, bend your right leg.

4. To push off, thrust against the ice with your right foot and unravel the slightly twisted position by rotating the arms counterclockwise. Your left arm should point in the direction of, and be parallel to, the line of flight. Your right arm should be parallel to the line of flight but be pointing away from the direction in which you are skating.

5. The placement of the left foot on the ice is the same as it was for the original push-off: perpendicular to the long axis and as close to the beginning of the thrust as possible. The right foot should be picked up in front, positioned about 12 inches from the skating foot. It is immediately obvious that the second push-off is the same as the first. However, since you will be skating across the ice with some speed, less time is available for the movement. The remainder of the edge is executed similarly, except that the movements are reversed.

BACK INSIDE EDGES

In skating, maneuvers that seem difficult at first become much easier with experience, and often ultimately seem easier than maneuvers that appeared to be quite simple at the outset. Less experienced skaters often find back inside edges easier to accomplish, while they find back outside edges more difficult. The more experienced skater, while not finding either difficult, will ultimately discover more applications for back outside edges and may eventually feel slightly more comfortable with them than with back inside edges—although the difference is only slight.

The Setup:

1. Stand two body lengths away from rinkside, facing the nearest barrier, away from the direction in which you will be skating.

2. Place your feet 12 to 18 inches apart, with your weight equally distributed between them.

3. Position your left arm in front of you, pointing toward the near barrier. Place your right arm to the side, pointing to the far end of the rink.

4. Remember the constants: Stand erect, chin up, and arms at a comfortable level above your waist but below your shoulders.

The push-off is the same as the push-off for back outside edges, except that the lean at the end of the push is in the direction of the thrusting foot instead of away from it. This alters the shape of the thrust on the ice, which is more or less straight at the beginning and curves more sharply at the end.

The Push-Off

1. Bend your knees.
2. Twist your body by rotating your arms and shoulders counterclockwise, while simultaneously raising your right foot and extending it across and behind your left leg. As the right foot lifts off the ice, shift your weight totally to the left leg.
3. Once in the twisted position, *push!* The push-off should be explosive. Unravel the twisted position by rotating your arms and shoulders clockwise as you press against the ice with your left foot, exerting pressure by straightening your left leg.
4. As the push progresses, lean back slightly and toward your left shoulder. This serves to prepare you to step on the inside edge as you place your right foot on the ice.
5. Place your right foot on the ice, perpendicular to the long axis. Be certain that your right leg is bent as the weight shifts onto the right foot.
6. Raise your left foot in front of you. It should be about 12 inches away from your skating foot, toe pointed and foot turned out. Straighten your left leg.
7. Your left arm should now be pointing toward the push-off spot, while your right arm should be placed behind you and to the side, at about a 45-degree angle to the line of flight.

The execution of a back inside edge will not seem mysterious after all you have done so far. The head movement will again be the only complexity and will improve as you become more skilled. As a beginner, you should try to hold your head in the original position (that is, facing the location of the push-off) until the rotation has begun. As the shoulders rotate, turn your head with them until you are looking back in the direction in which you are skating. When you become more adept, you will be able to turn your head to the inside of the circle immediately after the push-off, enabling you to see where you are skating. When you move your head immediately after the thrust, the danger is that you will disturb your position and your balance. One of the most common errors associated with rapid head movement is lifting or rolling the right shoulder forward. Try to avoid that, whether you are a beginner or an expert, and note

that beginners, in theory, avoid this problem by rotating the head in ⬚⬚⬚⬚⬚⬚
with the shoulders.

The Execution:

1. Once firmly on a right back inside edge, begin to rotate the a⬚⬚⬚ ⬚⬚⬚
shoulders counterclockwise. In the final position, the right arm is in fr⬚⬚⬚ ⬚⬚⬚
the left arm is behind and pointing in the direction that you are ska⬚⬚⬚.
2. Simultaneously bring the free foot from in front to a position in back,
in a smooth, slow motion that is coincident with the upper body rotation. As
the free foot moves, keep it close to the skating foot. It should eventually end
up about six inches behind the skating foot, and turned out, with the toe
pointed. The leg should be bent slightly.
3. To control the rotational momentum, try to keep your hips tucked
under your trunk and hold your left hip rigid as you bring your foot back. Do
not let your left hip open up, that is, swing back with the leg and foot.
4. During this motion, you can slightly straighten the skating leg.

At this stage, you will be returning to the long axis, where you will change
feet. The execution of the push-off involves the same technique, except that the
movements will be less exaggerated due to the speed across the ice and the need
for performing the push-off more rapidly.

The Transition:

1. When you are virtually at the long axis, begin to bring your left arm
forward and right arm back. This will initiate the twisting motion that will coil
the body for the push-off.
2. To draw yourself into the push-off, press your left leg across and behind
the right leg into the imaginary semicircle that is about to be skated.
3. Bend your right knee and twist a bit more.
4. From this point, the push-off is exactly the same as the original push-
off, except that the movements are in the opposite direction and with the
opposite feet.

Back inside edges are frequently used in skating to achieve a particular
purpose—speed when skating backward, as take-off edges on jumps, or as part
of pair moves. They are rarely used as positions for artistic purposes. However,
the skater who excels at them has a unique opportunity to bring a new level
of importance to this essential skating maneuver.

Pattern of the imprint on the ice produced by back inside edges.

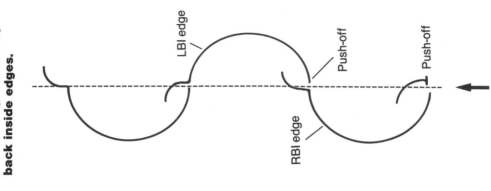

LBI edge

RBI edge

Push-off

Push-off

Direction of movement

At the long axis (see diagram), push off onto a left back inside edge (F).

Rotate your arms and shoulders counterclockwise, and pass your free foot back (E).

After the push-off, look into the circle, keeping your weight on the ball of your right foot (D).

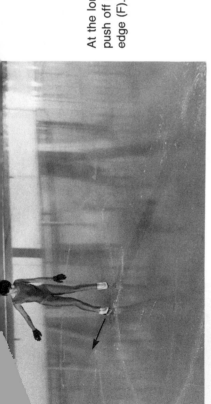

Back Inside Edges

Push off, shifting your weight to the right leg (C).

Wind up for the push-off (B).

To set up for a right back inside edge (shown here), face away from the direction in which you will skate. Position your left arm in front of you and your right arm to the side, keeping your weight evenly distributed between your two feet (A).

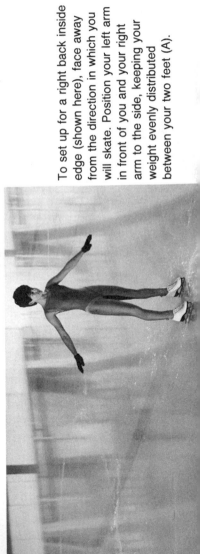

7

Turns

So, you now know quite a bit about how to skate forward and backward proficiently. However, the real trick is to be able to change rapidly from forward to backward skating, and from backward to forward. You can use two methods: one in which the skating foot stays the same, and one in which the skating foot and direction change simultaneously. The most important turns by far are those executed on one foot. Changing direction without switching feet is necessary for the execution of many maneuvers and will become an important feature of your footwork sequences and jump and spin preparations.

Four types of one-foot turns are available to the skater: the three-turn, the bracket, the counter, and the rocker. Each of these can be done from forward to backward, or backward to forward, and on either edge. There are two general types of two-foot turns: the Mohawk and the Choctaw. No one knows where the Indian names came from, but probably from an American-style skater of the 1880s. You employ two-foot turns only when changing from forward skating to backward skating. In figure skating, there is no terminology for changing feet while changing from backward to forward skating.

One-foot turns are generally introduced when a skater is learning compulsory figures, and they constitute an exceedingly important part of such figures. However, they can also be learned in preparation for free skating, independent of figures. The learning process for the two disciplines is somewhat different. For compulsory figures, the skater concentrates on the integrity of the edges and cusps (round-patterned edges leading into and out of the turn), the depth of the turn (how much the turn extends into or out of the circle), and its shape; in other words, the goal in figures is an exact drawing of a specific shape on the ice. In free skating, the object is to execute the turn in a way that is aesthetically pleasing, or congruent with the choreography of the program, and that prepares the skater for the next move. In free skating, the most commonly

Tracie Brown works on her turn maneuvers under the watchful guidance of the author.

employed turn is the three-turn. However, the skater must be competent in all the turns, since the other one-foot turns can provide variety and innovative touches to a skating routine. The methodology outlined below is derived, to a certain extent, from compulsory figures but is designed primarily to teach the turns to a skater who intends to use them in the context of free skating.

First, it is important to understand a number of general principles that apply to all turns.

PRINCIPLES

First, the principal driving force for a turn is the rotational, or angular, momentum of the upper body in concert, or at odds, with the inherent angular momentum of the edge of a blade on the ice. When in concert, the rotational momentum of the upper body on the approach to a turn proceeds at a faster rate than the rotational momentum exerted on the blade. At the point of maximum rotation, the blade is forced into a small curve, creating the first half of the turn. When at odds (that is, when the upper body is turning in a direction opposite to the lower body), the rotational momentum for the turn is created only by the upper body, and is only augmented by straightening the skating leg, by a shift of body weight to a different part of the blade, and by the tension at the waist created by the upper body and hips working against each other. At a precise moment during the preparation for the turn, the rotational momentum of the upper body overtakes that of the lower body (from the waist down) and forces the blade into a smaller curve, creating the entrance to a turn. This happens because the upper body is connected to and restricted by the lower part of the body at the waist. The tension created at the waist helps the skater both execute the turn and control the rotational momentum before and after the turn. This twisting or wringing sensation should be experienced by the skater in the fullest sense. If the upper body could spin freely around at the waist, a turn would be virtually impossible. The maximum point of rotation occurs when the shoulders are parallel to the skating foot. It is important to realize that the primary rotational force is exerted by the shoulders and that the arms merely serve to enhance shoulder rotation and help provide stability and balance.

Second, the entrance into a turn is enhanced by lifting over (straightening) the skating leg. This reduces the pressure (created by the skater's weight) of the blade against the ice.

Third, during the entrance into a turn, the weight is shifted from the part of the blade that is opposite the direction in which you are skating (back of the blade during forward entrances and front of the blade during back entrances) to the part of the blade that is the same as the direction of flight (front for forward skating and back for backward skating). This weight shift accelerates the entrance of the blade into the smaller curve of the turn.

Fourth, the rotation leading into the turn is checked to create the exit. A check consists of two opposing motions: the arms and shoulders rotating in one direction (the shoulders being the primary source of the check) and the hips rotating in the opposite direction. This opposing motion of the shoulders is begun prior to reaching the middle of the turn, since the check pulls the blade out of a path created by the rotation. The angular momentum that has built would merely result in the blade continuing to follow a curve with a small radius. The check pulls the blade out of that path and produces a turn. (More on the check in the discussion of specific turns.)

Fifth, the direction and degree of the body lean will determine the kind and shape of the turn. Before, during, and after three-turns and brackets, the lean remains into the circle on which the turn is executed. Before counters and rockers, the lean is into the circle skated in preparation for the turn; at the top of the turn, the lean shifts to a new circle on which the exit of the turn is executed.

Sixth, all turns are learned most easily when the skater is skating on a circle or semicircle, because the rotational momentum of that edge can be used by the skater to make the turn. However, once the technique is learned, turns can be approached from a multitude of preparations.

To simplify the descriptions, I shall give instructions only for turns on the right foot. I shall also only discuss Mohawks and Choctaws that begin on the right foot. However, you can and should execute all one-foot turns on either foot, and can and should enter Mohawks and Choctaws on either foot. To learn how to execute a turn on the left foot, simply reverse the direction of all the rotational instructions and use the directions for the right arm, shoulder, leg, and foot for the left, and vice versa.

THE THREE-TURN

The three-turn enables the skater to change from forward to backward skating, or vice versa, while simultaneously changing the edge from inside to outside or from outside to inside. The turn points into the center of the imaginary circle created by the edge on which the turn is executed. It is the easiest of turns to execute, since the rotation of the body is consonant with the inherent rotational force of the edge. The direction and the edge entering the turn dictate the name of the turn. For example, if the skater is gliding forward and is on an outside edge, the turn is called a forward outside three-turn. It is called a three-turn because its shape resembles the number 3.

The Forward Outside Three-Turn

This turn consists of a forward outside edge into the turn and back inside edge after the turn.

1. Set up as instructed for a right forward outside edge (see page 67).

2. Execute a right forward outside edge. The only difference now is that the free leg will remain behind throughout the preparation for the turn and after the turn. As the rotation begins, the free leg should be relaxed but extended back slightly and turned out. As the intensity of the rotation increases, the free leg will automatically turn outward less. However, you should not allow it to turn in since this will force the left hip forward, making it difficult to check the rotation on the exit. Your weight should remain on the back of the blade of the skating foot.

3. Throughout the turn, your head should face in the direction in which you are skating.

4. The clockwise rotation of the arms and shoulders will continue until you can no longer rotate. At this point, your shoulders will be parallel to the skating foot, your right arm behind and in line with the shoulders, and your left arm in front at a 90-degree angle to the skating foot. Once you reach that point, a number of movements will begin to happen at once.

Start by gliding forward on your right foot, then rotate clockwise for a right forward outside three-turn (shown here), keeping your free leg back in a relaxed position (A).

Rock to the ball of the skating foot as you enter the turn (B).

The Right Forward Outside Three-Turn

5. Allow your weight to roll from the back of the blade (heel of the foot) to the front of the blade (ball of the foot); lift (straighten) over your skating leg; begin to check the turn by rotating the arms and shoulders counterclockwise.

6. In the middle of the turn—the point at which you stop skating forward and begin skating backward and at which the edge changes from an outside to an inside edge—your skating leg should be straight, and you should be midway between rotation and the check. This is the point at which you should begin to think about bending the skating leg again.

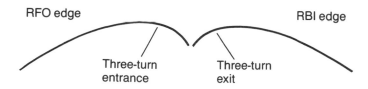

RFO edge   RBI edge

Three-turn entrance   Three-turn exit

Imprint on the ice resulting from a three-turn.
Note the shape—like a figure 3—and note, too, the change of edge at the top of the turn.

The edge change occurs at the top of the turn (C).

The free leg remains behind throughout the turn (D).

A strong check position (rotated counterclockwise) after the turn is the key to maintaining control (E).

7. As you bend the skating leg, take a little of the weight off the ball of the foot so that you are settled somewhere between the front and the center of the blade and on a back inside edge.

8. As you come out of the turn, your shoulders should be parallel to the skating foot, your right arm across the body at a 90-degree angle to the skating foot and the left arm pointing in the direction you are skating. The free leg should be turned out and extended back slightly.

The Forward Inside Three-Turn

This turn consists of a forward inside edge into the turn and a back outside edge out of the turn.

1. To execute a forward inside three-turn, set up as you would for a right forward inside edge (see page 72).

2. Do a right forward inside edge. The one difference is that you must keep your free leg behind as you rotate your arms and shoulders counterclockwise. As the rotation begins, your free leg should be extended slightly behind your skating leg and turned out gently. As the intensity of the rotation increases, the

The Right Forward Inside Three-Turn

Glide forward on your right inside edge, and rotate counterclockwise (A). As you execute the turn, rotate your arms and shoulders clockwise to check your body's rotation (B).

B   A

free hip will tend to rotate, or open up, and the free leg will inch across and behind the skating leg. Although this is permissible in free skating, the skater must control this motion. If the rotating motion of the leg and hip occurs without control, checking the rotation after the turn will be difficult. Remain on the back of the blade as you prepare for the turn.

3. Throughout the preparation and execution of the turn, you should be looking in the direction in which you are skating.

4. The counterclockwise rotation of the arms and shoulders should continue until you can rotate no longer. At this point your right arm will be in front, at a 90-degree angle with the skating foot, the left arm behind and parallel with the skating foot, and the shoulders parallel to the skating foot. As you approach this point, a number of movements should occur.

5. Straighten the skating leg. As you do so, shift the weight from the heel to the ball of the foot. When the skate begins to move into the turn, start to check the rotation by rotating your arms and shoulders clockwise.

6. At the top of the turn (the point at which the edge and direction change), begin to bend the skating leg and to shift the weight from the front to the center of the blade.

7. As you exit the turn, execute the check: left arm and shoulder perpendicular to the skating foot, right arm parallel to the skating foot, and shoulders parallel to the skating foot. The free leg should be bent, turned out slightly, and held about 12 inches directly behind the skating foot.

The Back Outside Three-Turn

This turn consists of a back outside edge into the turn and a forward inside edge out of the turn.

Although the back outside three-turn is not required for jump or spin preparations, it ranks as one of the most commonly used turns in connecting steps and footwork. To execute the back outside three-turn, set up the way you would for a right back outside edge (see page 74).

1. Like the preparation for the forward three-turns, the preparation for the back outside three-turn requires that the free leg remain in its original position following the push-off—in this case, in front and slightly turned out.

2. During the preparation, place the weight on the ball of the foot.

3. Rotate the arms and shoulders counterclockwise to the maximum position—the right arm perpendicular to the skating foot and the left arm and both shoulders parallel to the skating foot. As the rotation proceeds, you will be tempted to allow the free hip to rotate into an open position. While some

B   A

The Right Back Outside Three-Turn

Start by gliding backward on your right outside edge. Keep your free leg firmly in front as you rotate counterclockwise (A). Rotate your arms and shoulders clockwise to check the turn (B).

openness of the hips is helpful in preparing for the turn, losing control of the left hip will complicate the check after the turn.

4. As the rotation is reaching the maximum point, begin to straighten the skating leg. Rock from the ball of the foot to the heel. Initiate the checking action by rotating the arms and shoulders clockwise.

5. Throughout the turn, keep your head facing the direction in which you are skating.

6. At the top of the turn, begin bending the skating leg. Remain on the back of the blade during the exit from the turn.

7. After the turn, the shoulders and right arm should be parallel to the skating foot and the left arm should be across the body in front at about a 45-degree angle to the skating foot.

The Back Inside Three-Turn

This turn consists of a back inside edge into the turn and a forward outside edge out of the turn.

The back inside three-turn is also not commonly used in preparation for jumps and spins but is incorporated rather frequently into footwork sequences. The preparation for the right back inside three-turn uses the setup for the back inside edges, with two differences: First, instead of rotating counterclockwise after the push-off, the rotation is clockwise. Since, after the thrust, the shoulders and arms are already partway to the maximum rotational position, it is necessary only to rotate a bit more. This is somewhat difficult, because the rotational force of the edge contributes less to the motion. Second, at the beginning of the edge, the head faces forward, and at the end, it faces outside the circle.

1. During the preparation, keep your weight over the ball of the foot. Your free leg should be in front, slightly across the skating leg, virtually straight and turned out ever so slightly.

2. Rotate the arms and shoulders clockwise until they attain the maximum rotation—the shoulders and right arm parallel to the skating foot and the left arm at a 45-degree angle to the skating foot.

3. As the maximum position is approached, begin to straighten the skating leg, and rock from the front of the blade toward the back. In addition, begin the check by rotating your arms and shoulders counterclockwise.

4. At the top of the turn, it's time to think about bending the skating leg again.

The Right Back Inside Three-Turn

Start by gliding backward on the right inside edge, and rotate your arms and shoulders clockwise (A). To check the turn, rotate your arms and shoulders counterclockwise (B). Keep your free foot in front of you before, during, and after the turn.

A

B

5. After the turn, the shoulders and the left arm should be parallel to the skating foot, and the right arm should be in front of the body at a 45-degree angle.

BRACKETS

Brackets are turns that point out of, rather than into, the curve on which they are executed. Since the turn itself consists of edges that curve in a direction opposite to the curve of the circle (and also opposite to the inherent rotational direction of the edges of the bracket), the rotation required to produce the turn is, therefore, opposite to the rotational direction of the edge. For example, the inherent direction of rotation on a right forward outside edge is clockwise. By contrast, the entrance edge into a right forward outside bracket must curve in a direction opposite to the inherent curve of the circle. This means that the skater must rotate counterclockwise to create the entrance edge. This opposition has two effects. First, the bracket is slightly more difficult to execute than the three-turn, since the upper body is going against the natural rotation of the edge. Second, since the actual curvature of the cusps leading into and out of the turn is contrary to the natural rotational direction of the edge, it is difficult to execute a bracket at a high speed. As a result, skaters rarely use brackets in high-speed footwork sequences unless the skater jumps over the turn and doesn't actually allow the blade to draw the turn on the ice.

The Forward Outside Bracket

This turn consists of a forward outside edge into the turn, and a back inside edge out of the turn.

1. Use the same setup as you would for a right forward outside edge (see page 67).

2. After your push-off onto the forward outside edge, keep your left arm and shoulder in the original position. Begin to bring your right arm across and in front of your body. Place your left leg in front of your skating leg, with the free foot turned out and a few inches away from the skating foot. This will result in an open hip position, which is required to facilitate the contrary rotational motion.

3. As you approach the turn, rotate your left arm and your shoulders counterclockwise. The end point of the rotation will be reached when the shoulders and the left arm are parallel to the skating foot and the right arm is at a 90-degree angle to the skating foot.

4. Continue to look in the direction in which you are skating.

The Right Forward Outside Bracket

B   A

Glide forward on your right outside edge and rotate counterclockwise—that is, opposite to the inherent clockwise rotation of the edge. This prepares you for the turn (A). To check the turn, rotate clockwise and pass your free foot to the front (B).

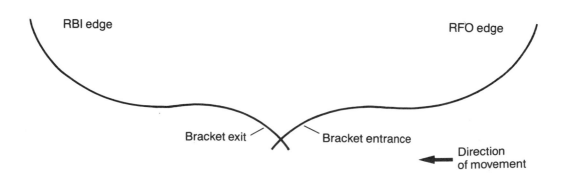

RBI edge   RFO edge

Bracket exit   Bracket entrance

Direction
of movement

Imprint on the ice resulting from a bracket.
The change of edge at the top of the turn produces a "rabbit-ears" pattern. Note the difference between the curve of the circle and the entrance and exit edges of the turn.

5. Just before the bracket, fairly abruptly straighten the skating leg and bring the free leg back into the circle. Since the time available for the turn is significantly shorter for the bracket than for the three-turn, you must straighten your skating knee that much faster. As you straighten the leg, rock from the heel of the foot to the ball and begin to check your shoulders and arms, rotating them clockwise.

6. At the top of the turn, your hips should gradually assume a closed position, provided that you do not allow the free hip to swing back as the turn is executed. Closing the hips is achieved by bringing the free leg forward. Its final position after the turn should be virtually straight in front of the skating foot, about 6 to 12 inches away. Begin to bend the skating leg.

7. As you exit the turn, your head no longer faces the direction of flight, but now faces the direction from which you have come. Remain on the ball of the foot. On the exit, your shoulders and right arm should be nearly parallel to the skating foot, while your left arm should be slightly across the front of the body.

The Forward Inside Bracket

This turn consists of a forward inside edge into the turn and a back outside edge out of the turn.

1. Set up for a right forward inside edge (see page 72).

2. After the thrust, keep your right arm and shoulder back, and place your weight on the back of the blade. Begin to bring your left arm across your body to increase the body's rotational momentum. Simultaneously, pass the free leg forward to a position about six inches from the skating foot. Turn the free leg out ever so slightly.

3. As you approach the turn, begin to increase the intensity of the clockwise rotation of your shoulders and arms. You should feel as though you are drawing your body to the turn with your free foot.

4. Look in the direction of flight before, during, and after the turn.

5. To start the turn, bring your free leg back to a position three to six inches behind the skating foot, where it will remain. Straighten the skating leg as abruptly as you did for the forward outside bracket. At the same time, rock from the heel to the ball of the foot and remain there during and after the turn.

6. As you enter the turn, begin the check with your shoulders and arms, rotating them counterclockwise. The hips should feel as if they have begun to rotate in a clockwise direction at the same rate of speed that the shoulders, moving in the opposite direction, are checking the turn.

7. At the top of the turn, begin to bend the skating leg.

The Right Forward Inside Bracket

Glide forward on your right inside edge and rotate clockwise (A).

Bring your free foot next to your skating foot just before executing the turn (B).

To check the turn, rotate your arms and shoulders counterclockwise and bring your free foot back (C).

8. After the turn, your shoulders and left arm should be parallel with your skating foot, the left arm pointing in the direction of flight. The right should be across the front of your body at about a 45-degree angle to the skating foot. The free foot, which is a few inches behind the heel of the skating foot, should be turned out so that it forms about a 45-degree angle with the skating foot.

The Back Outside Bracket

This turn consists of a back outside edge into the turn and a forward inside edge out of the turn.

1. Set up for a right back outside edge (see page 74).
2. After the thrust, maintain the beginning upper body position, which consists of the right arm and shoulder back and pointing in the direction of flight, and the left arm and shoulder in front. Throughout the turn, continue to look in the direction of flight. Prior to the turn, your head should be cocked slightly to the inside of the circle on which you are skating. After the turn, it should be cocked slightly to the outside. Remain on the ball of the foot.

3. Bring the free leg back, passing it alongside the skating foot. Place it about six inches directly behind the skating foot. Make certain that your hips are not in an open position and that your left hip does not begin to swing around with your shoulders.

4. To initiate the turn, bring your free leg in front of your skating foot, lifting the knee slightly. Fairly vigorously straighten the skating leg. Rock to the heel of the blade, remaining there after the turn.

5. As you are beginning to enter the turn, commence the checking motion. Rotate your shoulders and arms counterclockwise. The movement of the free leg forward during the initiation of the turn (step 4) starts the hip check, wherein the hips feel as if they are rotating in the opposite direction to the shoulders' rotation on the check.

6. At the top of the turn, begin to bend the skating leg, and bring your free leg back in a path perpendicular to the skating foot. The free foot and leg should finish perpendicular to and behind the skating leg. In fact, the free foot will hang slightly outside the imprint of the circle made on the ice by the blade of the skating foot.

7. After the turn, your shoulders and left arm should be parallel to the skating foot, and your right arm should be in front and across the body.

The Right Back Outside Bracket

To prepare, glide backward on your right outside edge. Rotate your arms and shoulders clockwise, keeping your free foot back (A). As you perform the turn, bring your free leg forward. To check the turn, rotate your arms and shoulders counterclockwise and pass the free leg back (B).

B   A

The Back Inside Bracket

This turn consists of a back inside edge into the turn and a forward outside edge out of the turn.

1. Set up for a right back inside edge (see page 79).

2. After the push-off, follow the instructions for the back inside edge. The method is exactly the same until immediately before the bracket.

3. Just prior to the bracket, intensify the counterclockwise rotation. At this point, the shoulders will be parallel with the skating foot, the left arm will be back and parallel with the skating foot, and the right arm will be in front and across the body at about a 90-degree angle to the skating foot. Your free foot should be behind the skating foot and turned out at a 90-degree angle to the skating foot.

4. Fairly aggressively straighten the skating leg and simultaneously lift the free leg, from the knee, up and to the center of the circle to help you over the turn. Rock from the front part of the blade to the back, remaining on the heel after the turn.

5. Throughout and after the turn, continue to look in the direction in which you are skating.

The Right Back Inside Bracket

To prepare, glide backward on your right inside edge and rotate the arms and shoulders counterclockwise (A). As you enter the turn, bring your free leg forward (B).

A

B

6. As the turn begins, start the check. The motion of the free leg, which helped initiate the turn, will also begin the hip check in a direction opposite to the clockwise motion of the check by the shoulders and arms.

7. Bend your skating leg at the top of the turn.

8. Following the turn, your left arm should be in front and across your body at a 45-degree angle to the skating foot. Your shoulders and right arm (which is back) will be parallel to the skating foot.

COUNTERS

Counters are a combination of a bracket and a three-turn: the entrance of the counter is a bracket, while a three-turn constitutes the exit from the turn. The principles that govern the preparation for brackets generally apply to the entrance into the counter. The principles that govern the three-turn apply to the exit from a counter. One important difference exists: Three-turns and brackets are executed on a single imaginary circle. Counters are executed on two circles, one for the preparation for and entrance into the turn, and another for the exit from the turn. Counters call upon yet another concept in skating, which is a change of lean in the middle of the turn. This phenomenon occurs in two jumps in skating: the Walley (see page 232) and the Lutz (see page 257). I must admit to having invented a variation on the Lutz that involves a bracket action rather than a counter-like action. In fact, it is the only jump in skating with a bracket-like motion. (More on this variation in the chapter on toe jumps, page 237.)

Three-turns and brackets involve a change of edge which occurs simultaneously with the change from forward to backward or backward to forward skating. However, with the counter, no such edge change occurs. Looking at the line of the properly executed counter turn left by the blade on a clean sheet of ice, one should detect no break in the line—proof that there has been no edge change.

The Forward Outside Counter

This turn consists of a forward outside edge into the turn and a back outside edge out of the turn.

1. For the preparation and entrance into a right forward outside counter, follow the instructions for the right forward outside bracket (see page 94).

2. The differences between the forward outside counter and the right forward outside bracket begin to appear at the top of the turn. Shift the

direction of your lean from the first circle to the second. Bring your free foot forward, placing it 6 to 12 inches in front of the skating foot, slightly turned out. Remain on the ball of the foot during and after the turn. Bend the skating leg.

3. Following the turn, your shoulders and right arm should be parallel with your skating foot, with the right arm pointing in the direction of flight. Your left arm should be across the front of your body at about a 45-degree angle to the line of flight. Continue to look in the direction of flight.

The Right Forward Outside Counter

To prepare, first establish forward motion on your right outside edge. Then rotate counter-clockwise and pass your free leg to the front (A). Bring the free leg back for the turn. To check the counter, rotate clockwise and pass the free leg to the front (B).

B

A

Imprint on the ice resulting from a counter.
Since no change of edge occurs at the top of the turn, there is neither a space nor a rabbit-ears pattern left on the ice.

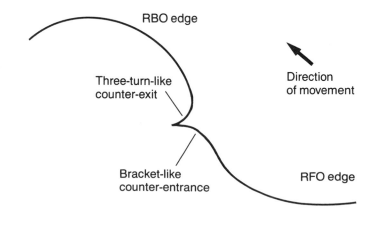

RBO edge

Three-turn-like counter-exit

Direction of movement

Bracket-like counter-entrance

RFO edge

The Forward Inside Counter

This turn consists of a forward inside edge into the turn and a back inside edge out of the turn.

1. For the preparation and entrance into a right forward inside counter, follow the instructions for the right forward inside bracket (see page 96).

2. At the top of the turn, change your lean toward the second circle, remaining on your inside edge as you do so. Bring your free leg forward and bend your skating leg. Remain on the ball of the foot. Continue to look in the direction of flight during and after the turn.

3. Following the turn, your free foot should be 6 to 12 inches in front of your skating foot and slightly turned out. Your shoulders and left arm should be parallel to your skating foot, with the arm pointing in the direction of flight. Your right arm should be across the front of your body, at about a 45-degree angle to the line of flight.

To prepare, skate forward on your right inside edge and rotate clockwise, extending your free leg in front (A).

The Right Forward Inside Counter

The Back Outside Counter

This turn consists of a back outside edge leading into the turn and a forward outside edge exiting the turn.

1. For the preparation and entrance into a right back outside counter, follow the instructions for a right back outside bracket (see page 97).

2. At the top of the turn, shift the direction of your lean from the first to the second circle while remaining on your outside edge. Aside from this difference, all else is virtually the same as the check on a right back outside bracket: Remain on the back of your blade, look in the direction of flight, achieve virtually the same check position in the upper body (though with slightly less exaggeration), and place your free foot behind your skating foot.

Bring your free foot to your skating foot as you enter the turn (B).

To check the turn, rotate your arms and shoulders counterclockwise and bring your free foot in front (C).

B A

The Back Outside Counter

To prepare, glide backward on your right outside edge and rotate your arms and shoulders clockwise, keeping your free foot behind (A). To help you execute the turn, bring your free leg forward on the turn entrance. Rotate your arms and shoulders counterclockwise and pass the free foot back (B).

The Back Inside Counter

This turn consists of a back inside edge leading into the turn and a forward inside edge exiting the turn.

1. For the preparation and entrance into a right back inside counter, follow the instructions for a right back inside bracket (see page 99).

2. At the top of the turn, shift your weight from the first circle to the second circle. The techniques for the check and exit are the same as those for the bracket, except for the position of the free foot after the turn, which is behind and slightly outside the circle following the counter.

The Back Inside Counter

A   B   C

To prepare, glide backward on your right inside edge and rotate your arms and shoulders counterclockwise (A). To execute the turn, bring your free leg next to your skating leg, straighten the skating leg, and rotate your arms and shoulders clockwise (B). On the exit of the turn, your left arm and shoulder should be in front, your right arm and shoulder back, and your free foot behind the skating foot (C).

ROCKERS

Rockers are another combination of three-turns and brackets: The entrance of the rocker is a three-turn, the exit is a bracket. The methods of preparing for a three-turn generally apply to the entrance for a rocker, while the methods of exiting from a bracket are generally those used in exiting the rocker. Like counters, rockers 1) are done on two circles, 2) require a change in the direction of lean from the first circle to the second circle at the top of the turn, and 3) do not involve a change of edge. Like counters, one uncommon jump exists that mimics the rocker action: the reverse inside Axel.

The Forward Outside Rocker

A   B   C

To prepare, glide forward on your right outside edge, pass the free (left) foot to the front, and rotate your arms and shoulders clockwise (A). To execute the rocker, bring the free foot behind (B). On the exit, check your rotation by rotating your arms and shoulders counter-clockwise and passing the free leg in front of you (C).

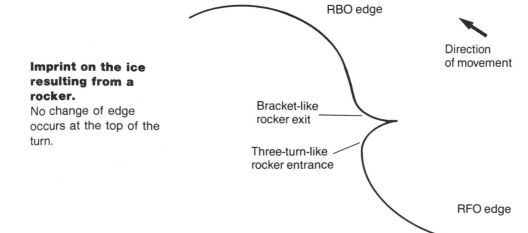

RBO edge

Direction
of movement

**Imprint on the ice
resulting from a
rocker.**
No change of edge
occurs at the top of the
turn.

Bracket-like
rocker exit

Three-turn-like
rocker entrance

RFO edge

The Forward Outside Rocker

This turn consists of a forward outside edge leading into the turn and a back outside edge leaving the turn.

1. For the preparation, follow the directions for a right forward outside edge (see page 67).

2. As you approach the long axis of the imaginary circle, intensify the clockwise rotation in the same way you would in preparing for a three-turn—that is, bringing the shoulders parallel to the skating foot, the left arm across the body, and the right arm back, slightly outside the area defined by the imprint on the ice.

3. Executing the turn involves a number of movements: Bring the free foot back; this movement should occur with the thigh virtually motionless and the lower leg moving like a pendulum. Straighten the skating leg. Shift the weight from the heel to the ball of the foot. Begin to shift the direction of the lean from the first circle to the second circle.

4. Near the top of the turn, begin the check by rotating your arms and shoulders counterclockwise. At the top of the turn, begin to bend the skating leg and also begin to bring the free foot forward. Most important, the shift in the direction of lean should occur at the midway point between the first and second circles; in other words, your body should be erect at that point.

5. The technique on the exit of the rocker is the same as that used for the exit from a forward inside bracket, but with one important difference: coming out of a rocker turn, the free leg is in front of the skating leg.

The Forward Inside Rocker

This turn consists of a forward inside edge leading into the turn and a back inside edge leaving the turn.

1. Prepare for the turn by executing a right forward inside edge (see page 72).

2. As you approach the turn, intensify the counterclockwise rotation as you would for a forward inside three-turn. That is, rotate the shoulders until they are parallel to the skating foot, bring the right arm across the body, and move the left arm back, slightly outside the imprint of the edge on the ice. The one difference is that the free leg remains in front of the skating leg.

3. To execute the turn, bring your free foot back as you did for the forward

outside rocker. Straighten the skating leg. Shift your weight from the heel to the ball of the foot. Begin to change the direction of your lean from the first to the second circle. Near the top of the turn, begin the check by rotating your arms and shoulders clockwise.

4. At the top of the turn, begin to bend your skating leg and also begin to bring your free foot forward. Since you are in the middle of shifting the direction of your lean from one circle to the next, your body should be erect at this point.

5. The technique on the exit of the turn is the same as that used for a forward outside bracket (see page 94).

The Forward Inside Rocker

To prepare, glide forward on your right inside edge, rotate your arms and shoulders counter-clockwise, and pass your free foot in front (A). Bring your free leg back for the turn. To check the turn, extend the free foot in front and rotate your arms and shoulders clockwise (B).

B   A

The Back Outside Rocker

This turn consists of a back outside edge leading into the turn and a forward outside edge leading out of the turn.

1. To prepare for the turn, use the technique for a back outside edge (see page 74). The only difference is that, once you bring your free foot back, keep it close to the skating foot and turned out at about a 90-degree angle to the line of flight. The rotation should be as intense as that required for a back outside three-turn (see page 91).

2. To execute the turn, straighten the skating leg. Rock from the ball of the foot to the heel. Bring your free leg forward slightly and lift it slightly by lifting the knee; this latter motion helps carry the body over the turn. Begin to change the direction of your lean from the first to the second circle. Initiate the check by rotating your arms and shoulders clockwise.

3. At the top of the turn, begin to bend your skating leg. Start to bring your free leg back.

4. Following the turn, use the technique for the exit from a back inside bracket (see page 99).

The Back Outside Rocker

To prepare, glide backward on your right outside edge, and rotate your arms and shoulders counterclockwise (A). To execute the turn, bring your free leg forward and rotate your arms and shoulders clockwise (B). To check the turn, pass your free leg back (C).

The Back Inside Rocker

This turn consists of a back inside edge leading into the turn and a forward inside edge leaving the turn.

1. To prepare for the turn, use the technique described for a right back inside three-turn (see page 92). Instead of leaving the free foot in front during the preparation for the turn, bring it back immediately after the thrust, placing it directly behind, about six inches away from the skating foot.

2. The only other differences between the entrance into a back inside three-turn and that into a back inside rocker are the change in direction of lean from the first to the second circle (which commences on the entrance into the rocker), and the movement of the free knee forward and upward on the entrance into the rocker. Initiate the check by rotating the arms and shoulders counterclockwise.

3. At the top of the turn, begin to bend the skating leg and to bring the free leg down and back. The body should be erect, with no lean for a split second at the top of the turn.

4. For the exit from the back inside rocker, use the technique for the exit from a back outside bracket (see page 97).

The Back Inside Rocker

To prepare, glide backward on your right inside edge and place your free foot behind you, in line with your skating foot. Your shoulders should be parallel to the skating foot, with your right arm and shoulder back, and your left arm and shoulder forward (A). To execute the rocker, lift your free leg forward (B). Then, to check the turn, rotate your arms and shoulders counterclockwise and bring your free foot behind you (C).

C

B

A

THE MOHAWK

The easiest and most useful two-foot turn is the inside Mohawk; the most difficult, the outside Mohawk. Controlling the Mohawk is a great deal easier than controlling the one-foot turn, since the alternation of feet provides greater stability as the turn occurs, and greater force on the check.

The Inside Mohawk

The inside Mohawk is basically a three-turn motion performed on two feet. It always begins and ends on an inside edge.

1. Push onto a right forward inside edge. (Although you can start an inside Mohawk on either foot, this discussion will pertain only to an inside Mohawk starting on the right foot.)

2. Rotate counterclockwise as you would on a normal inside edge leading into a right forward inside three-turn (see page 90).

3. As you rotate, remain on the back of the blade.

4. As you near completion of the rotation, bring your free foot to the skating foot, placing the heel of the free foot against the instep of the skating foot.

5. When you have reached maximum rotation, begin to check the rotation by turning your arms and shoulders clockwise, changing feet simultaneously with the check.

6. Once you've transferred your weight to the left back inside edge, extend your right leg behind you.

7. The final position of the arms and shoulders consists of the right arm and shoulder pointing in the direction of flight, the left arm at a 90-degree angle to the line of flight and to the inside of the imaginary circle, and the shoulder line parallel to the flight path.

8. Throughout the Mohawk, you should be looking in the direction in which you are skating.

Skaters use the inside Mohawk very frequently as part of their footwork, in preparation for jumps, and as part of jump take-offs, such as for a flip jump (more on flip jumps later). The technique described above is much more precise than that used by many skaters in a freestyle setting. As your proficiency improves, you will be able to reduce some of the rigidity in favor of other objectives: for example, assimilating the Mohawk into an overall footwork sequence, or for a change in body and leg positions in preparation for a jump.

The Inside Mohawk

  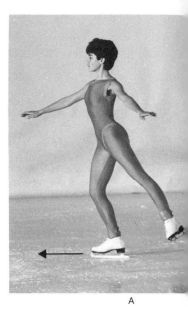

C   B   A

For a counterclockwise inside Mohawk (shown here), start by skating forward, and push onto a right forward inside edge (A). Rotate your arms and shoulders counterclockwise. Bring the heel of your left foot against the instep of your right foot (B). Shift your weight to your left foot and extend your right leg back (C).

Imprint on the ice resulting from a counterclockwise inside Mohawk.

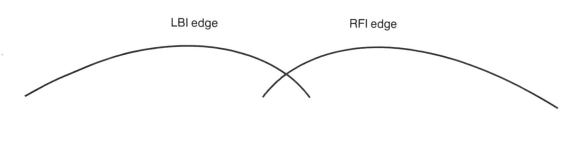

LBI edge   RFI edge

◀— Direction of movement

The Outside Mohawk

The outside Mohawk is far less common in freestyle skating, but it is an important turn in ice dancing. An outside Mohawk is simply a bracket turn performed on two feet.

1. Push onto a right forward outside edge.

2. Rotate counterclockwise as you would to prepare for a right outside bracket (see page 94).

3. Bring your left foot forward, with your weight on the heel of the skating foot. As you reach maximum rotation, bring your left foot back, placing the left instep against the heel of the right foot.

4. Almost simultaneously, slide your left foot onto the ice, shifting your weight from the right foot to the left back outside edge.

5. Check your turn by rotating your arms and shoulders clockwise. In the final arm and shoulder position, your right arm and shoulder point in the direction of flight, the left arm is at a 90-degree angle to the imprint on the ice and outside the imaginary circle, and the shoulder line is parallel to the flight path.

6. Throughout the outside Mohawk, it is useful, particularly on the check, to look in the direction in which you are skating.

Imprint on the ice resulting from a counterclockwise outside Mohawk.

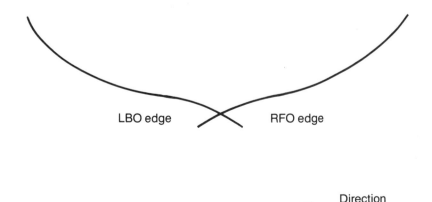

LBO edge   RFO edge

Direction
of movement

THE CHOCTAW

The Choctaw also resembles two types of single-foot turns: the rocker and the counter. For a rocker-like Choctaw, the entry edge is always a forward inside edge. The counter-like Choctaw is always begun on the forward outside edge. You will find that Choctaws are most frequently employed in compulsory dances and in free dance routines. Free skaters rarely employ Choctaws except in a footwork sequence or as a preparatory move for a Lutz jump (in the latter case, the rocker-like Choctaw would apply).

The Rocker-like Choctaw

The rocker-like Choctaw is approached only from a forward inside edge.

1. Push onto a right forward inside edge and execute the same motions used to prepare for a right forward inside rocker (page 107), but with one exception: Keep your left leg behind the skating leg, with the instep of the left foot against the heel of the skating foot and with your free leg turned out in an open position.

2. Instead of doing a turn at the point of maximum counterclockwise rotation, place your left foot on the ice and shift your weight from the right foot to the left back outside edge.

C

The Rocker-like Choctaw

To perform a rocker-like Choctaw entered from a right forward inside edge, rotate your arms and shoulders counterclockwise (A). As you prepare for the Choctaw, begin to lean out of the circle. Shift your weight to your left foot, keeping your right arm and shoulder firmly back (B). After the Choctaw, extend your free foot in front (C).

3. Lift the right foot in front and turn it out.

4. Check your arms and shoulders by rotating them clockwise, and place additional backward pressure on the leading right shoulder.

5. In the final arm and shoulder position, your right arm and shoulder point in the direction of flight, the left arm is at a 90-degree angle and outside the second imaginary circle, and the shoulders are parallel to the flight path.

6. Throughout the Choctaw, look in the direction you are skating.

Imprint on the ice resulting from a rocker-like Choctaw entered on a right forward inside edge.

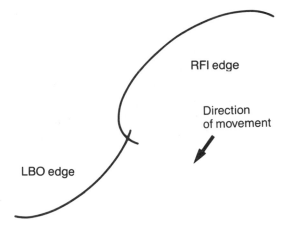

RFI edge

Direction of movement

LBO edge

B

A

The Counter-like Choctaw

A forward outside edge constitutes the only entrance into a counter-like Choctaw.

1. Push onto a right forward outside edge and prepare for the Choctaw in the same way you would set up for a right forward outside counter—rotating counterclockwise.

2. At the point at which you would execute a counter, bring your free foot back behind the skating foot, with the instep of the left foot passing by the heel of the right foot just before your shift your weight.

3. Transfer the weight from the heel of the right foot to the ball of the left foot on a back inside edge. Lift the right foot in front of the left foot as you make the weight transfer.

4. Check the Choctaw by rotating your arms and shoulders clockwise.

5. In the final upper body position, your right arm and shoulder point in the direction of flight, your left arm is at a 90-degree angle to the line of flight and inside the imaginary circle, and the shoulder line is parallel to the flight path.

6. Throughout the turn, look in the direction in which you are skating.

Imprint on the ice resulting from a counter-like Choctaw entered on a right forward outside edge.

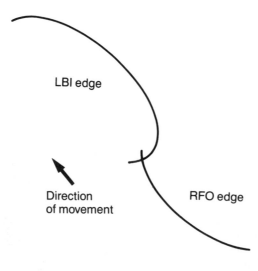

Practicing all the turns described here is essential if you're ever to become a competent skater. If you can't change directions quickly and easily, you'll be seriously hampered in your effort to attempt more difficult maneuvers. In addition, turns provide a method of learning how to control angular momentum, which governs every figure-skating technique.

8

Stopping and Falling

As much fun as it is learning to glide at increasing speeds and to change direction at a moment's notice, learning to stop is of equal importance. Avoiding high-speed collisions with other skaters and crashes into the barrier around the rink demands stopping skill and versatility. While many variations exist, every skater should know the three fundamental stops: the T-stop, the snowplow, and the hockey stop.

THE T-STOP

Learning a T-stop is best done in two stages. The first stage can be more accurately described as a "drag stop" and should be regarded as only a learning technique.

To begin, pick up some speed skating forward. Skate on two feet for a couple of seconds to gain your balance as you prepare for the drag. Place your left arm in front and your right arm to the side.

Now pick your left foot up behind your right foot and turn it out. As you glide on the flat of the right blade, drag the inside edge of the left blade on the ice, holding it about six inches behind the right foot to maintain your balance. Nearly all the weight should remain on the right foot.

As you come to a stop, the position of your upper body relative to your hips should remain constant. You can do this by pressing the right shoulder back slightly. The stability of the upper body position is one of the important requirements for a secure T-stop.

This learner's T-stop can and should be practiced on both feet. For stops in which you drag the right foot, merely reverse the above instructions.

119

No matter how good a skater you are, at one time or another you will fall.

The second step is to attempt the full-blown T-stop.

Pick up some speed, as you did for the learner's T-stop. The only difference now is how you place the dragging foot: The instep of the left foot should actually touch the heel of the right foot, and the weight should be placed on the left outside edge.

As your left foot touches the ice, shift most of your weight onto it. To ensure that you are on the outside edge, lean back slightly. If you catch an inside edge on the left foot, the blade will not slide along the ice perpendicular to the direction of flight, and this will force you to abort the stop. Adjusting the backward lean will help you find the position necessary to always hit the left outside edge.

The T-Stop

In preparation for a T-stop, push onto your left foot, letting your right leg become the trailing leg (A). As you place pressure on your right foot, lean back (B). The key to executing the stop properly is making sure your shoulders remain parallel to your right foot (C).

C   B   A

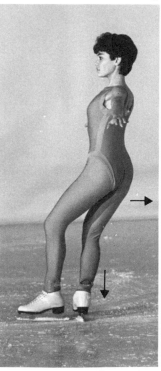

THE SNOWPLOW

If you have ever skied, you will know how to do a snowplow stop. The technique is virtually the same on the ice.

Once again, pick up some speed going forward. To prepare, glide on two feet, keeping your weight just barely on the inside edges and on the center of the blades. Keep your arms straight out at the side. To stop, bend your knees and begin to push your heels out away from each other, so that your feet become pigeon-toed. Leaning back ever so slightly will ensure that you remain on the inside edges.

The snowplow is an excellent beginner's stop. However, as you learn to skate faster, you will have to rely on the next stop, the hockey stop.

The Snowplow Stop

To execute a proper snowplow stop, simply bend your knees and pigeon your toes inward.

THE HOCKEY STOP

This stop and its many variations provide the most skilled skaters with the best way to brake forward motion.

To learn the hockey stop, use the same preparation that you used for the T-stop and the snowplow stop: Build up some forward speed, and then glide for a moment on both feet. Unlike those stops in which you move gradually into the stop, the hockey stop consists of a fairly abrupt motion. When you are ready, bring your feet together, bend your knees, and simultaneously swivel the shoulders in opposition to the hips; that is, rotate the shoulders clockwise and turn your feet and hips counterclockwise. Your feet and hips should end up perpendicular to the line of flight, while your torso should be facing the direction in which you are skating. Now lean back slightly, so that your right foot is on an inside edge and your left foot is on an outside edge. The more you bend your knees, the more pressure will be applied to the ice, and the faster you will come to a stop. This is not unlike a parallel stop on skis.

Once you have learned the hockey stop, you will quickly discover that many variations exist, some of which can be done on one foot.

All of these stops are useful when you are skating forward, but you might ask, "How do I stop when I am skating backward?" Hockey players frequently use a reverse snowplow, where the heels face each other and the toes point out. Figure skates have an excellent structure for stopping that hockey skates lack, a toe pick. When you are skating backward and suddenly need to stop quickly, bend your knees and dig the toe picks into the ice. This technique is most useful for emergency stops, but since it is not often employed, it has no official name.

The Hockey Stop

The hockey stop is performed with the feet parallel to each other and perpendicular to the line of flight. Your shoulders should be parallel to your feet and turned forward.

FALLING

Perhaps the most valuable skill that any skater can have is knowing how to fall properly and how to get up quickly. Unfortunately the best way to learn how to do this is to practice it. Fortunately, skating provides no shortage of opportunities!

Falling is an inevitable feature of learning how to skate. In fact, even the most experienced skaters fall. When you do not fall occasionally, it is time to evaluate your training routine. It often means that you have reached a peak and are no longer attempting to conquer more difficult maneuvers—you may be in danger of not advancing. On the other hand, this must be balanced against your primary objectives: to perfect technique, to eliminate falling, and to achieve consistency.

Still, at the outset, falling purposely has its benefits. At the very least, it can convince you not to be afraid of falling. This is extremely important if you are to avoid injuries. Furthermore, an intentional fall teaches you in the context of a controlled situation the best ways to break a fall. Accidental falls occur unexpectedly and require a split-second reaction. The more experience you have, the better your instinctive reaction will be when you need it.

In any fall, there are five points to remember: 1) Keep your head away from the ice; 2) break your fall with your hands; 3) if at all possible, try to land on your seat; 4) bend your knees to break the force of the fall; and 5) do not linger on the ice, but rise to your feet as quickly as possible. Remembering all of these in the midst of a fall may seem a tall order. However, some of these points will become automatic with practice, if they aren't from the outset. For example, from the beginning of my skating career, I instinctively used my hands and kept my head up when I fell—no doubt having learned that art as a small child on dry ground.

The key to practicing falls is to start gently.

Start by skating forward, not too fast. Bend your knees while simultaneously bending forward, and once you are close to the ice, fall sideways, making certain that your hands are reaching toward the ice to break your fall.

As you fall, let your legs slip out to the side and try to fall on your seat, avoiding your hipbone. Once you are on the ice, turn over on your hands and knees in a crawling position. Put one foot on the ice, and push up on that leg. Place the other foot on the ice as you stand up.

After you have practiced this technique a number of times, try to reduce the time between impact and the return to a standing position.

For the next exercise, try falling backward instead of sideways. Repeat the

Falling

When falling to the side, break the fall with your hands.

Make certain that you bend your knees and fall sideways when making a practice fall.

After a fall, remember to rise to your feet quickly from a crawl position.

same technique in all other respects. When practicing a backward fall, remember to fall on your seat. Once you are sitting on the ice, roll onto your back. To avoid hitting your head, place your chin on your chest. Get up the same way as you did on the sideways fall.

Finally, practice the same exercise but fall forward. In this case, you will want to be quite certain that you break the fall with your hands before your knees touch the ice. In all other respects, this exercise is the same.

When practicing all of these exercises, work on decreasing the time required for the entire maneuver as you become more and more competent. Ultimately this will result in a closer correspondence between a practice fall and the real thing. In addition, this will prepare you for fast recoveries—an essential element in any experienced skater's repertoire. In fact, in a competitive situation, an instantaneous recovery from an unfortunate fall can go a long way to minimizing the fall's negative impression on the judges and the audience.

9

Spins: General Principles and Positions

In Chapter 2, I mentioned that the physical principles of angular momentum—the combination of linear and rotational forces—govern skating. While this is certainly true for skating in general, it is in spins that the effect of angular momentum is greatest and most apparent. The success of a spin depends on the correct management of angular momentum. Since the rotational forces involved in spins are many times more powerful than the forces affecting stroking and edges, controlling them is a challenge and requires technical precision.

You will recall that angular momentum is forward motion along a curved path. On the entrance to a spin, you will be experiencing angular momentum. Once in the spin, angular momentum itself comes to a halt, and all linear force is translated into angular speed. You now are rotating around a fixed vertical axis which extends from the highest point of the body to the blade on the ice. The most important point on this vertical axis is the point at which the blade meets the ice. The absence of angular momentum means that fewer variables are involved in the execution of a spin (or, as physicists say, fewer vectors are influencing the resulting motion). Therefore, provided the center of gravity, or balance, is maintained, spins should be less difficult to execute than jumps, for example.

In spins, the primary objective is to rotate rapidly, which means that the skater must increase angular speed, or rotations per minute. This is accomplished quite simply by reducing the distance of the parts of the body from the vertical axis. In other words, the faster you wish to spin, the more you will bring your arms and free leg in line with the vertical axis, close to the body. In addition, since the true center of gravity is at the point where the blade meets the ice, you will also lower your arms and free leg toward that point. As you increase the speed of a spin, the force generated is outward and upward, the path of least resistance. If you allow the force to follow the path of least

127

Successful spins depend on correctly managing
angular momentum.

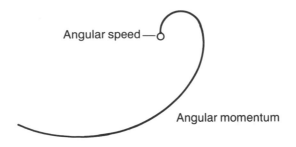

Angular momentum and angular speed.
Angular momentum governs a spin's entrance edge, while angular speed is the main force affecting the spin itself.

resistance, you lose some of the force that contributes to rotational speed. Therefore, when increasing the speed of a spin, you must work your arms and free leg inward and downward. The precise method by which this is accomplished will vary from spin to spin.

The translation of angular momentum into angular speed around a fixed vertical axis, which occurs at the point of transition from the entrance to the spin itself, has important implications for the best method of entering a spin. First, the translation of one force into another is difficult to control. Second, the benefit from a successful translation of fast linear motion (which produces great force) into fast rotational motion is marginal: fast forward motion cannot be efficiently converted into fast angular speed. As a result of these considerations, building up speed for an entrance into a spin is generally considered inadvisable and a waste of energy. A slow entrance will achieve the same results and is likely to result in greater consistency.

For purposes of this discussion, I shall describe spins only in the counterclockwise direction. The predominant direction in which you jump should be the direction in which you spin. Since most people execute jumps in the counterclockwise direction, as a beginner you should assume that you will also find this the best for you. If you have strong left-handed tendencies, however, jumping and spinning in the clockwise direction may work better for you.

One reason you want consistency in your predominant direction of rotation relates to the issue of dizziness. When you spin, your eyes focus on an immobile object, following it until the object passes beyond peripheral vision.

The eyes then race ahead to focus on a new object. This means that when spinning counterclockwise, your eyes are moving slowly to the right during the focus and rapidly to the left for the new object. In clockwise rotation, the eye motion is the opposite. At the end of the spin, your eyes continue to move in this pattern, creating a sensation of dizziness. With a great deal of practice, your eyes will return to normal quickly, and you can eventually avoid dizziness altogether. Training the eyes to function effectively in both directions would take a great deal of time, more time than the skater has to devote to this problem—particularly when more important tasks are at hand, such as conquering the next triple or quadruple jump or increasing the speed of his or her spins. However, the fact that you jump predominantly in one direction does not mean that you can't or shouldn't do spins or jumps the other way. It can be done and has been done quite effectively by Toller Cranston and John Curry, as well as by myself.

There are basically two types of spins: forward and backward. Forward counterclockwise spins occur on a left back inside edge and are entered by a left forward outside edge and three-turn. Back counterclockwise spins occur on a right back outside edge and are entered by a right forward inside edge and three-turn.

Two basic techniques are used for the great majority of spins. While exceptions exist, the underlying principles are important to remember, regardless of the adaptations.

THE PREPARATION

The first technique pertains to the preparation for the spin. The most common preparatory edge before the entrance edge of a forward spin is a right back inside edge—although advanced skaters employ a wide range of preparations and certain spins require special entrances. To arrive on the back inside edge, skate back crossovers, clockwise, to gain some speed. When you cross the right leg over the left, you will be on a right back inside edge. As you take that edge, very slightly rotate your arms and shoulders in the clockwise direction. Extend your left leg across and behind the right leg, which should bend deeply. The radius of the back inside edge will be quite small. Continue to look in the direction in which you are skating. You can use this preparation for most spins. Slight variations, important to certain spins, are described in the sections on those spins.

Preparation for entrance into a basic counter-clockwise forward spin.
The most common preparation for entrance into a counter-clockwise forward spin is from a right back inside edge. A deeply bent right knee is essential.

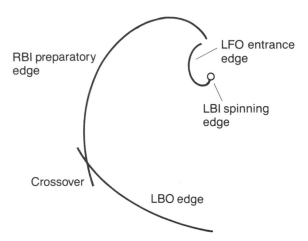

The pattern followed for a conventional entrance into a forward spin.

RBI preparatory edge

LFO entrance edge

LBI spinning edge

Crossover

LBO edge

The most common preparation for a back spin consists of three stages: a left forward inside edge, a right forward inside edge, and a right forward inside three-turn into the spin. Execute a left forward inside edge as described on page 72. At the end of the edge, switch feet. This transition is slightly different from the one used on basic forward inside edges. Place the right foot on the ice 18 to 24 inches away from the left foot—a wide step. As you shift your weight to the right foot, bend your right leg. Rotate your arms and shoulders counter-clockwise until they are parallel to the skating foot. Pick up the left foot and

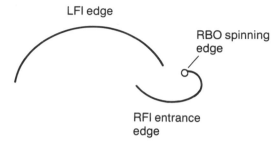

LFI edge

RBO spinning
edge

RFI entrance
edge

The pattern followed for a typical entrance into a back spin.

extend the left leg back and to the inside of the imaginary circle created by the right forward inside edge. As the edge progresses, allow your free leg to swing back around the skating leg, in a wide arc. Lean slightly forward and to the center of the imaginary circle. This will create an edge with a small radius. Look in the direction in which you are skating. All of these motions will create the rotational momentum necessary to do the three-turn and commence the spin.

THE EXIT

The second general technique involves the exit edge. The exit from a forward spin often involves a change of feet, although not always. Exits from back spins generally do not require a change of feet.

When a change of feet is involved, the technique is as follows. At the end of a spin on the left foot, bring the right foot to the left toe. Turn the right toe in slightly. Simultaneously slow the rotation by opening the arms out to the side in the basic arm position. Bend the left leg and push onto a back right outside edge, sinking into a deep right knee bend. Immediately extend the left leg behind you with your knee locked and your toe pointed. Be certain that you do not raise your left hip as you extend your left leg back. Keep your left arm slightly in front and your right arm to the side, perpendicular to the line of flight. Arch your back and hold your chin up, looking slightly to the right. Hold the edge at least for a five count.

If the spin ends on the right foot and requires no change of feet for the exit, the technique is somewhat different. The most important and useful exit of this type is the one from a fast-back upright spin. Although the final position for all spins ending on the right foot may not be exactly the same as that for a fast-back upright spin, the general principles governing the exit will be the same. The final position in the spin itself consists of a straight left leg

Typical Change-of-Feet Exit from a Back Spin

In this example, Brian Boitano completes a back spin on his left foot (A). To prepare for his exit on a right back outside edge, he lifts his right foot slightly and slows his rotation by opening his arms to the basic arm position (B). He then transfers his weight to his right leg as he pushes off with his left foot (C). His actual exit position is open—his arms are out, his left leg is extended behind him, and his right leg is deeply bent (D).

A

crossed in front of a straight right (skating) leg, with the legs together. The arms are straight down, close to the body, the hands joined in front of the lower abdomen.

From this position, the exit occurs in two stages, and all of the movements in each of the two stages occur simultaneously. To begin breaking the rotational speed of the spin, bring your hands up to your chest, lifting your elbows out to the side, with your arms parallel to the ice. Lift your left leg at the knee, keeping the left foot crossed over and close to the right leg. You'll be tempted to bend your right leg at this point. Don't—doing so will only confuse you on jumps later, since the exits on spins and the landings on jumps are virtually identical.

The next stage is the exit itself. Uncross your left leg. Open your arms out to the basic position, with your left arm slightly in front. Extend your left leg straight back and sink into a deep right knee bend. The final position of the left leg should be the same as in the change-of-feet exit: knee locked, leg turned out, and toe pointed. Hold the position for at least five seconds. Arch your back and look proud.

This one-foot exit from a fast-back upright spin is perhaps the most important checking motion you will learn in skating. It almost precisely mimics the correct technique for breaking the rotation in the last split-second of a jump in preparation for the landing. Practicing this check repeatedly will reward you many times over on jump landings. Try to do it as fast and as accurately as possible, and make sure that you hold the back outside edge for a five count.

Again, there are many exit variations for spins. However, the ones just described are universal and provide other benefits for the skater, such as training for solid technique on jump landings, a method of straightening the right leg, and a simple way to practice controlling rotational speed.

B

C

D

Typical Back-Spin Exit Requiring No Change of Feet

To exit a basic back spin (A) without transferring weight from one foot to the other, raise your free leg and your arms, with your hands out in front of you (B). Extend your left leg back to pull yourself onto a back outside edge, and assume an open position (C).

A

B

C

10

Basic Spins

Several basic spins comprise the primary repertoire of a skater: the two-foot spin, the fast-forward and the fast-back upright spins, the cross-foot spin, the sit spin, the camel spin, and the layback spin. Over the years, skaters have created a multitude of variations on these spins through changes in body position, combinations of the basic spins, and the addition of a jump into, or in the middle of, a basic spin. Variations in the body position on basic spins will be described in the instruction for each spin. Spins with jumps, known as flying spins, and spin combinations will be covered in subsequent chapters.

The goal in most spins is to rotate as fast as possible, to have a pleasing and well-defined body position, to maintain absolute balance before, during, and after the spin, and to spin in one place. The latter point, known as centering the spin, will ring in your ears repeatedly as you learn to spin. Mastering these basic spins is important for a number of reasons:

1. The more you spin, the more accustomed you become to the sensation of rotating.

2. The faster you spin, the more accustomed you become to the rotating sensation that you will experience in jumps.

3. When you are able to break out of a fast spin just after you reach the peak rotations per minute, you will be better able to stop the rotation coming out of a jump.

4. Certain spins, such as sit spins, strengthen your back and legs in a way that will contribute to strong stroking and powerful jumps.

5. Spins represent an important element of a competitive free-skating routine and must be included if you want to achieve high marks in technical merit.

135

Spinning in place—known as "centering" a spin—is one of spinning's more difficult aspects. Here, Debi Thomas centers her sit spin perfectly.

In addition to those points, remember that skating is a spectator sport, and for the spectator, a well-executed spin is exciting to watch. In fact, it is so exciting that Ed Sullivan invited Ronnie Robertson, the 1956 Olympic Silver Medalist, to appear on his television show to demonstrate that Ronnie could spin faster than an electric fan. It was quite impressive!

THE TWO-FOOT SPIN

You can and should learn how to do a two-foot spin at an early stage in your development as a skater. The primary objective of this spin is to experience the sensation of spinning in one place. Although you will try to spin as fast as you can, rotating rapidly in a two-foot spin is neither easy nor particularly important. Balance and technique should occupy most of your attention.

    The two-foot spin consists of three essential parts and one optional part. The three essential parts are the setup, the windup, and the spin. What is optional is the exit. You can either rotate in the closed spinning position until you come to a stop, or you can exit on a back outside edge, using the change-of-feet version described on page 131.

The Setup:
Place your feet parallel to each other, 12 to 18 inches apart, with your weight equally distributed. You should be standing on your blades' inside edges. Hold your right arm in front and your left arm to the side. Keep your shoulders and hips square—that is, perpendicular to your feet. Look straight ahead.

The Windup:
During the entire windup, keep your feet firmly planted on the ice. Rotate your arms and shoulders clockwise until your left arm is across your chest, your right arm is back, and your shoulders are parallel with your feet. Bend both your knees as you rotate, allowing a small amount of extra weight to be placed on the right foot. Look to the right.

The Spin:
To begin the spin, unwind and twist vigorously by rotating your arms and shoulders counterclockwise. Since you will now begin spinning in one place—your feet no longer stationary on the ice—your shoulders and arms will not pass much beyond the square position. Whip your head back, toward your left shoulder.

    As you bring your arms around, close them in toward the body, joining your hands. There are two possible final positions for the arms: one in which the elbows remain up and out to the side, with the arms parallel to the ice, and one in which the elbows are down and pressed against the side of the body in a prayer-like position. Both of these positions can be used in jumps and should be practiced at this point.

As you spin, straighten your knees and bring your feet together, until they are four to five inches apart. This resembles the motion used for sculling but is executed in a much more vigorous fashion. Your weight should be on the center to the back of the blades.

Allow the rotations to continue as long as possible, allowing the spin to run down to a stop of its own accord. If you wish to stop the spin before then, simply extend your arms out to the side and execute a conventional back outside edge exit, using the two-foot technique.

The Two-Foot Spin

From the set-up position for a two-foot spin (A), a strong windup is essential (B). Bend your knees as you rotate into the windup position. Initiate the two-foot spin by rotating your arms rapidly counterclockwise, straightening your knees, and bringing your feet together (C).

A

B

C

THE FAST-BACK UPRIGHT SPIN

As the name suggests, the back spin consists of fast rotations. However, at the outset, a slow back spin is permissible and useful. Speed will come with practice and increasing expertise.

The preparation for the back spin is described on page 129. At the point on the right forward inside edge when you are just about to lose control of the edge, do an inside three-turn. Remember to rock to the ball of the foot on the three-turn. Following the three-turn, you will be skating on a back outside edge and on the ball of the foot; the toe pick should not be touching the ice at this point. Nor should you be moving across the ice, but rather skating in one place, skating tiny circles about two to three inches in diameter on a back outside edge. This is accomplished in two ways. First, the deep right forward inside edge coupled with the wide backward swinging motion of the free leg enables you to translate angular momentum into angular speed. Second, the technique after the three-turn, described below, is designed to eliminate linear motion.

The Three-Turn:

Following the three-turn, stand straight over the skate. It will feel as if you are flipping your body over your free hip in an effort to try to catch up with the free leg. This is made easier by turning your left hip out, placing the free leg in front and bending it slightly, and holding the thigh parallel to the ice and the left foot no lower than the right knee. Straighten your skating leg on the exit of the three-turn. Virtually all lean will cease, except for a slight tendency to lean toward the right shoulder. Place your arms straight out to the side. Your shoulders and hips should be perpendicular to the skating foot. Look over your left shoulder.

The Acceleration:

Once you have your balance and have centered the spin, it's time to accelerate your angular speed. All of the following movements occur deliberately and continuously. Bring your left foot to your right knee without dropping the left thigh. The left foot will be crossed over the right knee slightly. Bring the hands in toward the bottom of the sternum (the bone that is in the center of the chest and ends at the abdomen). Join the hands at the sternum. Make certain that your elbows don't lift during this motion, and that your shoulders remain still. As your speed increases, the little circles you are making will become even smaller, and the tendency to lean toward the right shoulder will diminish almost totally. The toe pick on your right blade should be just grazing the ice but not digging into it. You are now midway through the spin.

To increase the speed of the spin even more, pass your left foot down the outside of the right leg, pressing the left heel down as you do this. Push your hands down the front of your body. In the final position, the legs are straight and close together, and the arms are tight against the body. Just before you begin to slow down, exit the spin using the one-foot method (see page 131).

The Fast-Back Upright Spin

The most important objective at the beginning of a basic back upright spin is to secure your balance. Extending your arms out, raising your free leg at the knee, and remaining on the ball of the skating foot make that goal attainable (A). The speed of the spin increases as your arms and free leg are brought toward your body and down (B).

A

B

The basic back spin is perhaps the most important spin in skating. The position toward the end of the spin resembles the position assumed in the middle of a jump. Practicing this position will help you immeasurably when you begin to attempt double, triple, and quadruple jumps. Furthermore, the action on the exit from this spin is the one you will use on the landing of most jumps. Practice this spin frequently, no matter how good you are. I have yet to find a skater who overpracticed the basic fast-back upright spin.

Common Errors When Performing the Fast-Back Spin

A slow spin is caused by:

- pressing the right toe pick too firmly against the ice;
- allowing the arms and/or shoulders to rise as they are pulled into the body;
- not pressing on the heel of the free foot as it descends;
- skating a preparatory forward inside edge that is not sufficiently deep;
- not waiting long enough before doing the three-turn into the spin.

A spin that is not centered is caused by:

- executing the forward inside three-turn too early, before the rotational momentum on the edge gains enough force to facilitate the translation of forward motion into angular speed;
- bending forward on the forward inside edge leading into the turn;
- not standing straight after the turn, thereby allowing the forward motion to continue;
- not turning the free hip and free leg out sufficiently;
- not holding the free leg high enough;
- holding the arms too high at the beginning of the spin.

Another very common error that has no immediate effect on the spin itself is a slow exit motion with the free leg swinging wide. Unless you strive to exit this spin with speed and agility, many of the benefits pertinent to your jumps that can be derived from the fast-back upright spin are lost.

THE FAST-FORWARD UPRIGHT SPIN

This may well be the most exciting basic spin in skating. On the fast-forward upright spin, skaters can attain unbelievable speed. This is the spin that Ronnie Robertson did on the *Ed Sullivan Show.* Because it is so exciting, it is not uncommon to see a fast-forward spin at the end of a program.

To enter this spin, use the back inside preparation edge, as described on page 129. Prior to the step into the spin, reverse the inherent clockwise rotation by pressing your left shoulder back. This will make it easier to center the spin—the most important goal. Many skaters have a tendency to rotate strongly counterclockwise on the preparatory edge in order to increase rotational speed by unwinding the position. This may gain a marginal increase in the speed at the beginning of the spin, but the disadvantages far outweigh the advantages. The primary drawback is that this preparation makes it harder to center the spin. Another problem, though less critical, is that the speed dissipates quickly until the arms and legs are pulled in. Therefore it is better to assume a somewhat open position prior to the step.

The Step:

The placement of the step is critical to centering the spin consistently. The optimal place to step is in the center of the imaginary circle created by the right back inside edge. To do this, you almost have to step forward in the direction you have come from. This is nearly impossible but is worth striving for because it reduces forward motion, making it easier to center the spin. By definition, you cannot center a spin if there is forward motion.

To do the step, reach with your left foot, heel first, into the center of the imaginary circle created by the right back inside edge. The step should be as wide as possible. The deeper you bend in the right knee, the wider the step will be. Lean forward as you step, keeping your back arched. Your shoulders should be perpendicular to your skating foot, with some backward pressure on the left shoulder. Keep the arms more or less out to the side, with the left arm slightly back. Step, with a bent left knee, on the left forward outside edge.

The Entrance:

The entrance edge itself must be as short as possible. This is accomplished by straightening the left leg vigorously. Do not lock the knee, but rather keep it bent ever so slightly. Bring the right leg around in a wide arc to a position in front of the skating leg. The position of the right leg should be the mirror image of the left leg at the beginning of the fast-back upright spin: thigh parallel to the ice, a slight bend in the knee, the right foot level with the left knee and extended out in front of the left leg. During this motion, apply additional backward pressure on your left arm and shoulder and look over your left shoulder.

The entrance edge ends at the point that a forward outside three-turn is executed. This places you on a left back inside edge, laying down tiny circles,

A   B   C

The Fast-Forward Upright Spin

The step into a basic fast-forward upright spin should be wide (A). Once into the spin, extend your arms out, lift your free leg in front of you at the knee, and keep your weight on the ball of your foot for balance (B). To accelerate the speed of rotation, bring your arms and free leg in toward your body (C).

two or three inches in diameter, on the ice. Your weight should be on the ball of the foot, the toe pick just grazing the ice surface. At this point your arms should be straight out to the side and perpendicular to the skating foot. Your right hip will be slightly down. Look straight ahead.

To pick up speed on the spin, follow the instructions given for the fast-back upright spin, reversing left and right. The key to the spin is the downward contraction into the rotation position.

Common Errors When Performing the Fast-Forward Spin

A slow spin is caused by:

- raising your shoulders and arms as you pull in;
- forgetting to press on the heel of the free foot as the leg passes down;
- exerting too much pressure on the ice with the toe pick;
- rocking on the blade;
- dropping the thigh as the free foot is brought to the skating leg;
- not pulling the arms and free leg in tight at the end of the spin, thereby losing some of the force needed to accelerate the rotational speed.

A spin that is not centered is caused by:

- stepping outside the imaginary circle created by the preparatory edge;
- remaining too long on the entrance edge, making it difficult to convert angular momentum into rotational momentum (angular speed);
- rocking on the blade;
- not lifting the free leg high enough at the beginning of the spin;
- an insufficiently wide step from the preparatory edge to the entrance edge;
- an insufficiently wide swing of the free leg on the entrance edge.

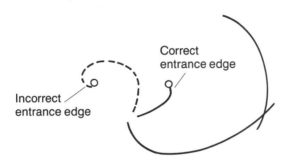

Correct and incorrect entrance edges for the basic fast-forward upright spin.
Stepping into the center of the circle created by the preparation edge enables you to efficiently convert angular momentum into rotational motion. Stepping out of the circle will produce an incorrect imprint on the ice.

THE CROSS-FOOT SPIN

The cross-foot spin is a spin on two feet. Unlike the two-foot spin you learned as a beginner, the cross-foot spin challenges the experts. Furthermore, you can achieve high speeds with this spin.

You can enter this spin in a number of different ways: from a two-foot spin, from a forward upright spin through a basic two-foot spin into the cross-foot spin, or from a back upright spin. The best way to learn the cross-foot spin is by executing the first part of a fast-forward upright spin. Then, where you would normally begin to bring your arms and free leg into the closed position, place your right foot on the ice, 6 to 12 inches from your left foot, and leave your arms out to the side. Make certain that your weight is distributed equally on the center part of both blades. You should be spinning on a left back inside edge and a right forward inside edge, and your knees should be bent. To cross the feet, shift a bit of your weight to the right foot and allow your left foot to cross in front of the right. Strictly speaking, you will be doing a bracket on the left foot. The left foot and leg turn out as the crossover evolves. Place a little pressure on your left shoulder, so that it feels as though it is leading the way. Look over your left shoulder.

Once the left foot is crossed over the right, begin to contract your arms into a closed position, just as you would on a fast-forward upright spin, to create speed. As you bring your arms in, straighten the legs. From this point on, the arm technique is the same as that for the forward upright spin.

To conclude the spin, pick up the right foot to uncross the legs, and push with the left back inside edge onto a right back outside edge.

THE SIT SPIN

Jackson Haines of New York, the American champion in 1863 and 1864 and often cited as the father of modern figure skating, has been credited with inventing the sit spin. In fact, it is occasionally referred to in documents of the International Skating Union, the official governing body for figure and speed skating, as the Jackson Haines spin. It is one of the oldest maneuvers in figure skating.

The sit spin represents one of the most important spins in skating, and when practiced often, it produces many benefits for the skater. Unfortunately skaters frequently regard the sit spin with disdain, for a number of reasons. First, the sit spin is difficult to learn. Second, it requires a fair level of energy. Third, the sensation of doing a sit spin cannot compare to the exhilarating feeling experienced, for instance, when executing a high floating Axel jump (see Chapter 14). Nevertheless, practicing the sit spin yields immense rewards which will become clear momentarily.

Its name tells you exactly what the sit spin entails: a spin in a sitting position. The kinds of sitting positions adopted by different skaters are diverse, and the choice of a particular position can sometimes be determined by convenience rather than by aesthetic design or technical objectives. I will describe the position that provides the skater with the most benefits technically, and then mention some other positions that may be adopted for choreographic or aesthetic reasons.

There are two methods of executing a sit spin: one that is useful when you are first learning the spin, and one that you can adopt when you have gained a fair level of competence.

Method for the Beginner

To prepare for the sit spin, use the basic method for a forward spin, described on page 129. Keep in mind that the general principles affecting your ability to center the spin are the same for the sit spin as they are for the fast-forward upright spin. From this point on, however, the technique is different.

The Step:

From the right back inside edge, step onto a left forward outside edge, bending your left knee deeply. Pick your right foot off the ice and extend it behind you. Lean forward over the skate, keeping your back arched and your chin up. As you step, press your left arm and shoulder back and reach across your body with your right arm. At this stage of the learning process, the length of your entrance edge is not critical.

The Spin:

Following the three-turn, which places you on the spinning (left back inside) edge, bring your free leg around and hold it in front of you. It should be turned out and slightly bent at the knee. Simultaneously with the free leg motion, bend your left leg as far as possible; the upper part of the leg should form about a 45-degree angle with the lower part of the leg. As your free leg comes around, release the backward pressure on your left shoulder and square your shoulders with your hips. Your arms should be relaxed, and ideally should assume a comfortable position, with your hands resting on the shin of your right leg. Throughout this movement, continue to lean forward while keeping your back arched and chin up.

Once in the spin, enjoy it for as long as you can. As in the case of upright spins, your weight is centered on the ball of the foot from the three-turn to the end of the spin.

The Exit:

As the spin begins to decelerate, rise out of the sitting position. This is quite simple if done correctly: Slowly straighten your left leg, keeping your back arched as you rise. Gradually bring your right foot in toward the skating leg,

A   B

The Sit Spin

At the entrance into the spit spin, let your free leg extend as far behind you as possible (A). That will allow you to pass the free leg on a wide arc as you move into the sitting position (B).

until it is finally touching your left knee, as described for the fast-forward upright spin. Your arms can be raised and opened to the same position that is used at the beginning of a fast-forward upright spin. In fact, the sit spin can be concluded with a fast-forward upright spin.

Method for the Expert

The expert can make several refinements that will 1) increase the speed of rotation on the spin, 2) heighten the excitement of the spin at the end, and 3) introduce positions that will generally benefit the skater's strength and style.

The first difference occurs on the preparation edge. Instead of allowing the shoulders and arms to rotate clockwise on the right back inside edge, keep your left shoulder and arm back and your right shoulder and arm in front. As you approach the step, bend your right knee even more.

To prepare for the step, pass your left leg from behind the right to the inside of the circle created by the right back inside edge. Rather than simply stepping on the entrance edge, reach into the circle with your left foot, heel first, to produce as wide a step as possible. Step onto a deeply bent left leg. As you do this, press your left arm and shoulder back farther and reach across your body with your right arm. You will have to lean farther forward over the skate than you did in the beginner method. A substantial amount of energy should be put behind these arm and shoulder positions. The rationale for this type of transition is to leave the right leg as far behind the left as possible. As objects move farther from their vertical axis of rotation, they produce greater force at any given speed of rotation at the vertical axis. In other words, if you spin at a constant speed, an object three feet away from you will travel farther in a second than it will if it is one foot away. The farther away, the greater the force.

This force is used to create a faster spin and comes into play as the right leg comes around on the entrance edge. Additional force is created by reducing the length of the entrance edge. A shorter entrance edge gives the right leg less time to come around, meaning that it must travel faster to arrive at its final sit-spin position. To avoid disturbing your balance, do not change the degree of bend in your skating knee as your free leg comes around.

As you do the three-turn, assume the sitting position as quickly as possible. If you can bring your arms into position with lightning speed, the spin will achieve even greater rotations per minute. Remember to keep your back arched and your chin up throughout the sit spin.

When you begin to decelerate, it is time to once again increase the speed of the spin. This produces what has become known as a "killer sit spin," so named because it requires a bucketful of energy, can cause pain if practiced often, and is perfected only with repeated attempts. The technique was developed by the famous coach of champions Gustav Lussi.

The essence of the "killer" technique is to rise into the final position of a fast-forward upright spin while coming up from the sitting position. It sounds simple enough, so try it. The first point is that you must rise out of the sitting position very, very slowly. Second, throughout the rising motion you must push your hips forward (tuck them under) very, very hard. If your hips are not tucked under, the killer will fizzle. Third, the arms must close in slowly, with the hands coming in to the stomach. Fourth, the free foot must begin to move toward the ankle of the left leg. Finally, you must press your chin in without lowering or raising it. Properly executed, these movements will produce a spin with speed that will surprise you.

From the "killer" will emerge many benefits, the most important of which is becoming accustomed to the correct position for jump take-offs. As you will learn in the chapters on jumps, one of the most important technical requirements is maintaining an arched back on the jump take-off as you lean forward and bend for the spring into the air. The sit spin trains your body to assume that position automatically. In the midst of a jump that requires split-second timing, it is immeasurably useful to know that one aspect of the technique is automatic!

VARIATIONS ON THE BASIC SIT SPIN

In an effort to be creative, skaters have invented an array of different sitting positions. This should be encouraged and is welcomed by most spectators. To describe all of the variations would require at least an entire chapter, but two frequently used positions warrant comment.

The first represents only a slight variation of the basic method. It consists of bending the left leg to its maximum. In order to accomplish this, you must relinquish your arched back in favor of a hunched position and keep your right leg straight. This basic position forms the foundation for many of the other variations.

While this approach is commonly utilized in the sit spin, you should be forewarned about its drawbacks. First, the deep knee bend required can exert undesirable pressure on the knee ligaments. When the hamstring muscles press against the calf muscles, it is like a lever that is pressuring the knee to open up. Over an extended period of time, this can result in a weakened knee, in some cases leading to a serious injury. To avoid this hazard, it is important to prevent the hamstring muscles from pressing against the calf muscles. You do this by halting the knee bend just before it reaches the maximum—a move that requires exquisite control and strong legs.

When the sitting position is executed on a fully bent skating leg, the free leg is straight and turned out, and the back rounds slightly.

Second, the hunched back makes no contribution to achieving correct body positions. Hunching is acceptable as long as the basic sit spin with arched back, described above, is practiced frequently.

Finally, it's next to impossible to execute a "killer" from this position, so the training benefits of the "killer" are lost.

The broken-leg sit spin is another familiar variation. This consists of a totally different free leg position: the free leg is turned in, bent, and held at the side. To assume this position, you must adapt your entrance. Step onto a slightly straighter left leg, making the entrance edge a bit longer. Go down into the sitting position more slowly, bringing your free leg around only as far as your side. You have substantial flexibility to create your own arm positions during the spin.

Only a few skaters incorporate the broken-leg sit spin in their programs, the most notable of whom is Toller Cranston of Canada, who uses the spin quite effectively.

Common Errors When Performing the Sit Spin

A slow spin is caused by:

- too much pressure on the toe pick during the spin;
- rocking on the blade from the heel to the ball of the foot;
- not centering the spin;
- not bringing the arms and free leg into the sitting position fast enough after the three-turn;
- not swinging the free leg wide enough on the entrance;
- remaining on the entrance leg too long.

A spin that is not centered is caused by:

- lowering your chin during the spin;
- rocking on the blade;
- not stepping into the center of the circle created by the preparatory edge.

An insufficiently wide swing of the free leg is caused by:

- not stepping wide enough on the transition from the preparatory edge to the entrance edge;
- not putting enough backward pressure on the left arm and shoulder and not reaching far enough across with the right arm;
- not stepping into the circle created by the preparatory edge.

A slow "killer" is caused by:

- not tucking your hips under as you come up from the sitting position;
- allowing your arms or free leg to move away from the body as you rise from the sitting position;
- permitting your head to droop.

THE BACK SIT SPIN

The back sit spin is merely a fast-back spin in a sitting position. In fact, the preparation is precisely the same as it is for the fast-back upright spin. The only difference occurs immediately after the three-turn: Instead of remaining on a nearly straight right leg, bend into the sitting position.

The most common problem encountered when learning this spin relates more to timing than to technique. However, one type of error is fairly common; that is, the flip of the body over the free hip may not be timed properly. As a rough estimation, the flip over the hip should occur immediately after the three-turn. In the absence of highly sophisticated computerized video equipment to study your technique, correction of this problem is merely a matter of practice. It is generally more common for skaters to flip too late rather than too early.

THE FORWARD CAMEL SPIN

Cecelia Colledge, an elegant skater from Great Britain, the 1937 World Ladies Champion and the first woman to do a double jump—the double Salchow—invented the camel spin. It was first performed in 1935 and at that time was appropriately called the "parallel spin." The camel is one of several skating moves that have been borrowed directly from ballet and adapted to the ice. Ballet's arabesque is the position that forms the basis for the camel spin.

To prepare for the camel spin, follow the basic method for all forward spins, described on page 129. The first difference occurs on the step.

The Step:

As you step, lean forward with an arched back and your chin up. Your upper body should be nearly parallel to the ice. Keep your left arm in front of you during the step. The actual step onto the left forward outside edge is wide and directed toward the center of the circle created by the right back inside edge. Press the right shoulder down slightly to avoid leaning too severely to the left.

The Entrance:

On the entrance edge, maintain the body and arm positions established during the step. To help create the rotation for the three-turn into the spin, bring your left arm around and back. It will feel as though you are reaching forward with the left hand and drawing a large horizontal circle in the air. Keep the right leg back and the left leg bent throughout the entrance. The entrance edge on this spin will last longer than it does for the forward sit spin or fast-forward upright spin. In fact, delay the three-turn until you are forced by the rotational momentum to do it.

The Spin:

On the exit of the three-turn, straighten the skating leg, rising up into the spin. At the same time, lift the free leg (which has been trailing behind fairly close to the ice) behind you, parallel to the ice. Turn the free leg out, lock the knee, and point the toe. This movement can throw you onto the toe pick. To counteract the upward force of the free leg, raise your head up. The head is your balancing rudder. The back should be arched, with the head and free foot being at about the same level.

The position of the arms is almost totally a matter of preference. For simplicity at the outset, place your arms out to the side like a gliding seagull. If the line of your shoulder is parallel to the ice and your arms are level, you should be balanced.

The Camel Spin

The preparatory position for the camel spin should be open (A). Step into the center of the circle and lean forward (B). Once into the spin, arch your back, lock both knees, point the free toe, and raise your chin (C).

A

B

C

The Exit:

For purposes of training, it is useful to conclude this spin with a fast-forward upright spin. The transition from the camel position to the upright position is fairly simple: While you bring your body into the upright position, swing your free leg around in front of your skating leg. During this movement, make certain the free leg is as fully extended as possible. The position at the end of the transition is the same as the beginning position for the basic fast-forward upright spin: right leg extended in front, knee slightly bent, right foot level with left knee.

Common Errors When Performing the Forward Camel Spin

A slow spin is caused by:

- excessive pressure on the toe pick during the spin;
- straightening the skating leg too slowly following the three-turn;
- an insufficiently wide swing of the free leg on the entrance edge;
- stepping outside the circle or not wide enough on the step;
- not leading with the left arm;
- a long entrance edge or one with a large radius.

Spinning on the toe pick is caused by:

- the head drooping during the spin;
- lifting the free leg too high without exerting counteracting pressure by arching the back and keeping the chin up;
- not locking the camel position in place with a solidly arched back, a firmly held free leg, and constant upward pressure on the chin.

A spin that is not centered is caused by:

- rocking on the blade;
- stepping outside the circle created by the preparatory edge;
- an entrance edge with a large radius, making it difficult to convert forward momentum into rotational momentum.

THE BACK CAMEL SPIN

The back camel spin is executed on the right foot and is merely a back spin in a camel position. However, there are a number of important differences in technique between the back camel spin and the fast-back upright spin.

The Preparation:

The pre-preparatory edge, as in the fast-back spin, is a left forward inside edge. Place your left arm and shoulder in front and your right arm and shoulder back. Stretch your free leg in front, about two to three feet from the skating leg and about a foot above the ice. The skating leg can be bent slightly.

On the transition to the preparatory (right forward inside) edge, place your right foot on the ice to the side, about two feet from your left foot. As you transfer your weight to the right foot, pick your left foot up to the side. Almost instantaneously, rotate your arms and shoulders counterclockwise. Lean forward, with your back arched and chin up.

The right forward inside preparatory edge should be short, with a small radius. Such a deep edge will allow you to translate forward momentum into rotational momentum. Swing your free leg wide and behind. This will force the forward inside three-turn.

The Spin:

Once you have done the three-turn, assume the camel position by holding the free leg behind and up; turn the leg out, lock the knee, and point the toe. As the free leg moves into position, raise your chin. These movements occur simultaneously but not instantaneously—rather, smoothly throughout the entrance into the spin. You will now be spinning on a right back outside edge and on the ball of your foot.

The Basic Back Camel Position

The basic back camel position is the same as the forward camel position, except that the spin is performed on the other foot.

The Exit:

To leave the camel position, raise your upper body, flipping it over the left hip as you did on the three-turn into the fast-back upright spin. Lower the free leg slightly, bringing it in front to the opening position for a fast-back upright spin, and conclude with that spin.

THE FORWARD LAYBACK SPIN

Cecelia Colledge, the inventor of the camel spin, also invented the layback, and it has long been associated with women's skating. However, male skaters have begun to incorporate this spin in their programs, giving it a decidedly stronger, more masculine flavor. Aside from its contribution to the attainment of a strong and limber back, it has little other training value. Skaters include the layback spin in competitive programs for two reasons: to increase the technical content of their programs and to answer choreographic needs.

The Preparation:

The preparation for and the entrance into the layback spin are the same as those for the fast-forward upright spin. Once in the spin, keep the free leg at a 45-degree angle to the side, turned out, and relatively straight. Keep your arms out to the side.

The Spin:

Before moving into the layback position, make certain that the spin is centered. Then bring your free leg back, turning your foot over so that the instep is facing the ice. Keep your free hip open by lifting at the knee. As you begin to tilt your upper body back, raise your chest. This will prevent your back from sinking into your hips, thereby pushing the hips into an incorrect position. Lead the movement with your head. As you tilt back, counteract this movement by lifting the free leg behind you; lead this leg movement with the foot and the lower part of your leg. Keep the free leg turned out from the hip. It should seem as though the knee is lifting and turning out. When you have reached the layback position, the lower part of the free leg and the foot should be parallel to the ice.

You are free to invent arm positions and movements in the layback spin. When you are first learning the spin, keep it simple by placing the arms next to the body and turned out, so that the palms are facing forward. A dramatic example of creativity on the layback is the "Beilman": Denise Beilman of

A   B

The Forward Layback Spin

Viewed from above, a layback is a thing of beauty (A). Correct positioning of the free leg and graceful arms are essential to a proper layback (B).

Switzerland, the 1981 World Ladies Champion, invented a variation that consists of grabbing the right foot with the right hand, pulling it to the back of the head, and with both hands lifting the foot above the head. This crowd-pleasing spin requires great control and a very limber back.

Common Errors When Performing the Forward Layback Spin

The most common error when performing a layback spin relates to the position and is more often a question of aesthetics. If the free hip is not turned out sufficiently, the free leg can take on a rather ugly appearance in the midst of the spin. While this was observed frequently at higher-level competitions several years ago, at the 1988 Olympics a poor free leg on a layback spin was rare.

The only other major error consists of allowing your back to sink into your hips as you tilt back into the layback position. This produces a less attractive position and, as you can guess, is not good for the back. To avoid this, simply lift your chest.

11

Flying Spins

A flying spin is a combination of a jump and a spin. The jump occurs at the beginning of the spin and is part of the entrance into it. When done well, flying spins are very appealing to an audience and can be thrilling for the skater as well.

Several general principles apply to flying spins. First, as in the case of basic spins, the angular momentum on the entrance must be converted into pure rotational momentum. In ordinary jumps, angular momentum enables the skater to travel a long distance across the ice, as well as high into the air. On a flying spin, the principles governing the spin dominate the jump portion. In fact, the object is to minimize forward motion on the jump portion of a flying spin.

Second, although creating speed on the spin portion remains a goal, it is not the only one. In absolute terms, the flying spin will never achieve the speed characteristic of a basic spin. This is because some of the forces assigned to achieving speed in a basic spin must be used to achieve height on the jump portion of the flying spin.

Third, centering the spin after the jump is dependent on converting all the angular momentum into rotational momentum. If the conversion has not occurred before the take-off, you will find it extremely difficult to convert it successfully when you hit the ice, spinning, after the jump.

Flying spins are not difficult for skaters with solid basic-spin technique and good jumping ability. Compared to many other moves in skating, learning a flying spin (of course, at the appropriate point in the development of your skating skills) will require far less practice.

157

The flying camel is one of the most exciting flying spins.

THE FLYING CAMEL

The flying camel consists of a jump from a left forward outside edge, approximately one revolution in the air, and a landing in a back camel spin, which, as described on page 152, is done on a right back outside edge. It is thought that the first skater to perform this maneuver was the great Dick Button, and consequently it is also known as the "Button camel."

The best way to learn the flying camel is to use a two-step preparation. The primary objective of this preparation is to set in motion a series of forces that will enhance the conversion of linear momentum into rotational momentum. To accomplish this, the preparation provides an almost linear path around which the body can set up rotational forces.

The Preparation:

Step, with a slightly bent knee, onto a left forward inside edge that has very little curve to it. Place your left arm and shoulder in front of you and your right arm and shoulder behind you. Position your free leg, which is straight, in front and slightly to the side, that is, to the inside of the circle created by the left forward inside edge. Stand erect, looking in the direction in which you are skating.

The step onto the second edge, a right forward inside edge, involves a wide step similar to the one you employed on the preparation for the back camel. One important difference is that the right forward inside edge also should have very little curve to it.

As you make the step, bring your left arm and shoulder back and your right arm and shoulder forward; lift your left foot off the ice and hold it to the side and slightly back; once securely on the edge, continue to rotate your shoulders and arms counterclockwise, and try to prevent a decrease in the radius of the edge. When your right arm is extended across your body and your left arm is fully back, do a right forward inside three-turn (it will feel as if you have to force the turn). As you do the three-turn, check it hard by rotating your arms and shoulders clockwise. In the final position, your right arm and shoulder should be back and your left arm and shoulder forward, your head should be turned over your right shoulder, and your left leg should be back. This position, which feels somewhat awkward and twisted, allows you to unleash a torrent of rotational force on the entrance edge.

The Step:

Once you are in this twisted position, it is time to prepare for the step into the flying camel. Look over your left shoulder, and rotate your upper body slightly, counterclockwise, bending forward and arching your back as you do. Step to the side onto a left forward outside edge; this edge should be at a 90-degree angle to the right edge. Stepping in this direction permits you to allow the right leg to move behind and across the left leg to the maximum, so that it is in an ideal position to create maximum rotational momentum as it comes around. Bend your left leg deeply, and as you shift your weight to the left foot, allow your right leg to glide behind the left leg—in much the same way as for the step into the basic forward camel spin.

As you step, your body lunge should increase until your upper body is parallel to the ice; to do this, you will have to press your right shoulder down (remember to keep the back arched and chin up). This downward pressure on the shoulder is important for two reasons: 1) it will prevent you from leaning too far into the circle created by the left forward outside edge, thereby decreasing the possibility of losing the edge and falling; and 2) it places you in a position for the back camel spin, precluding the need to find your balance after the jump (step). Your left arm and shoulder should be in front, and your right arm and shoulder should be back.

The action on the entrance edge requires excellent timing and involves a fairly complicated motion for what is often perceived as an easy spin. Regrettably, most skaters adopt a much more straightforward technique on the entrance edge and consequently execute less than brilliant flying camel spins. One reason for the lack of attention to technical detail is that most skaters can do the flying camel without adopting the ideal technique. However, for reasons discussed under "Common Errors," not adopting the optimal method can result in disaster and certainly will result in a less than perfect flying camel.

The Entrance:

As soon as you have made the step, swing your left arm back, counterclockwise, in an arc parallel to the ice. Wait one to two seconds, and then swing your right arm around counterclockwise, also in an arc parallel to the ice. Swing your free leg around, its motion slightly trailing that of the right arm, and step across in front of the left leg, which should not straighten fully on the entrance edge. As you step across the print, you may find yourself executing a half-turn on the left toe pick. This is both acceptable and desirable. The back spin should take place outside of the imaginary circle created by the left forward outside edge; stepping across the imprint of the entrance edge accomplishes this. The flying part should not actually be a jump but rather a step. In fact, the faster and smoother the change of feet, the more secure the spin and the faster it will be.

A B C

F G

The Flying Camel

The flying camel begins with the skater traveling on his left inside edge (A). A strong arm and shoulder position—left arm and shoulder forward, right arm and shoulder back—is critical. To start the transition to the preparation edge for the flying camel, the skater lowers his arms in front and starts to shift his weight to his free (right) skate (B). Once on the right forward inside edge leading into the three-turn, the skater rotates counterclockwise to the maximum (C). As he makes the three-turn, the skater checks it hard by rotating strongly clockwise (D). This creates the forces necessary for a powerful take-off. Now the skater leans forward as he steps onto the take-off edge (E), and his free leg and right arm come around simultaneously just before the stepover into the spin (F, G, H). As his right foot touches down, the skater swings his left leg around into the camel position (I).

D

E

H

I

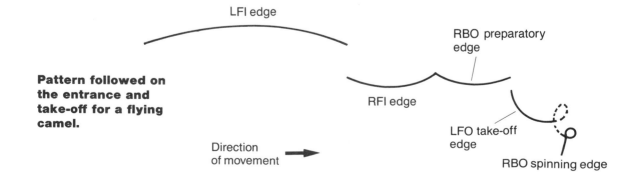

Pattern followed on the entrance and take-off for a flying camel.

LFI edge

RBO preparatory edge

RFI edge

LFO take-off edge

RBO spinning edge

Direction of movement →

The timing on this motion can be counted as beats, with two beats taking up one second:

Beats		Maneuver
Step	—	Step onto left forward outside edge;
One	—	left arm swings back;
Two	—	position held;
Three	—	position held;
Four	—	right arm comes around;
Five	—	step onto right foot.

The Spin:

As your weight shifts to your right leg, bend your right knee slightly to cushion the transfer; then immediately come up on a straight knee. Once your weight is on your right foot, simply swing your free leg around, counterclockwise, until it is back, high, and straight. Lock the knee. This position is merely the basic back camel spin position. As such, you will be spinning on the ball of your right foot. Throughout the flying camel spin, it is essential to keep your chin up and your back arched.

Common Errors When Performing the Flying Camel

A slow back camel spin, and one that is not centered, is caused by:

- assuming the back camel position too slowly following the step;
- not keeping the back arched, chin up, and free leg locked after the step;
- lifting the upper body during the entrance edge and the step;
- poor timing on the entrance edge;
- not stepping across the entrance edge on the step into the back camel;
- jumping on the transition from the entrance edge to the back camel spin;
- stepping in the direction in which you are skating instead of at a 90-degree angle to it;
- not twisting with sufficient force during the preparation.

A back camel spin that does not occur on the outside of the circle created by the forward left outside edge is caused by:

- incorrect timing of the arm motion on the entrance edge;
- not bringing the right arm around on the entrance edge;

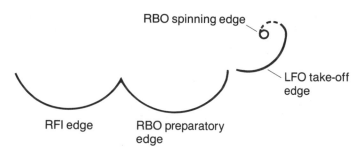

Direction of movement

RBO spinning edge

LFO take-off edge

RFI edge

RBO preparatory edge

A common error when performing the flying camel.
The pattern of the preparation phase of the flying camel should not show deep edges. If you fail to step across the take-off edge on the jump phase of the maneuver, the spin will occur in the circle created by the take-off edge—and that's wrong technique.

- not consciously stepping across the entrance edge on the jump part;
- not being sufficiently twisted on the back outside preparatory edge.

An actual fall or a feeling of almost losing the edge on the entrance edge is caused by:

- the left shoulder being down during the entrance edge because of insufficient downward pressure on the right shoulder;
- the path of the left arm on the entrance being downward;
- the body being upright and therefore leaning to the left.

While other errors can occur, such as not pointing your toes in the back camel or not keeping your back arched on the back camel spin, most others relate to aesthetic points rather than to technical problems.

THE FLYING SIT SPIN

The flying sit spin was first done by pupils of Gustav Lussi. Buddy Vaughn and Bill Grimditch are thought to have been the first practitioners, but it was Dick Button and Ronnie Robertson who made it famous. The flying sit spin consists of a take-off from a left forward outside edge, a sit spin position in the air during one and a half revolutions, and a landing in a forward sit spin. When the jump is high, it can be an exhilarating maneuver for skater and audience alike.

The Preparation:

The best way to approach a flying sit spin is from back crossovers. Moderate speed is acceptable and even desirable. Converting angular momentum into rotational momentum is accomplished relatively easily by the nature of the take-off edge. In this important aspect, the principles governing flying sit spins differ from those governing flying camel spins.

After executing a couple of back crossovers in the clockwise direction, step onto a right back inside edge. As you cross your right foot over your left to accomplish this step, begin to rotate your arms and shoulders clockwise. (Normally, on clockwise back crossovers, your left arm and shoulder are back and your right arm and shoulder are in front.) The clockwise rotation of the arms and shoulders should be smooth but strong—the left arm and shoulder ending up in front and the right arm and shoulder to the side. As this rotation occurs, bend your skating knee deeply and extend your left leg across and behind your right leg.

From this somewhat twisted position, you are ready to initiate the preparation for the step into the flying sit spin. The preparation edge and the take-off edge should form a mirror image of an S-curve. This preparation requires several simultaneous movements: Rotate your arms and shoulders counterclockwise; partially straighten your right knee; from its extended position relax the left leg so that it is almost hanging behind the right leg. Look in the direction in which you are about to step.

The Step:

The step itself is a critical element in the flying sit spin. Just prior to the step, bring your arms in front so that they are stretched out and pointing to the side. Several simultaneous movements occur as you step onto the left forward outside edge: Lean forward, with your back arched, chin up; bring your arms down toward your sides; deeply bend your left leg; and extend the free (right) leg behind and almost across the edge being skated.

The Take-Off:

From this point, you will bring your arms back to the front. At the same time, bring your right leg around. The pathway of the free leg determines whether or not angular momentum will be successfully converted to rotational momentum. Bringing the free leg around, not through, is essential. As the leg comes around, bring your arms forward and straighten your left leg to effect the jump. Toward the end of the edge, before lift-off, the impression on the ice will change from a clean edge to a skid.

For the position on lift-off, your left knee is straight; arms are in front, slightly open, hands no higher than the top of your head; your right leg is out to the side and parallel to the ice; and your body is upright.

After lift-off, bend your left leg fully, lifting it toward your chin, knee first. This will produce the illusion of great height since the maximum possible clearance between the left foot and the ice will result. Be sure the right leg is out to the side—do not bring it in front as you would on a basic sit spin. The time to prepare for the landing is at the peak of the jump. Landing is quite simple. The only movement required is straightening the left leg, which places it in a position to cushion the downward force of the landing.

The Landing:

The landing itself requires speed and agility. In fact, the faster the landing movements are executed, the faster the sit spin will be. You will land on a left back inside edge, spinning. As your left foot touches the ice, simultaneously bend your left leg, bring the right leg in front into a basic sit spin position, and bring your arms in front and rest your hands on your right shin. Keep your chin up. You should now, quite happily, be doing a basic forward sit spin. Since you travel a small distance in the air—that is, the point of touchdown is a foot or two from the point of take-off—your arm and leg movements are essential to centering the spin. From here, you can choose how to conclude the sit spin.

Several important principles bear noting. First, the mirror-image "S" curve preparation establishes forces that counteract linear momentum, enabling the conversion of all forces into rotational momentum. Second, the concerted movements on lift-off must be powerful and explosive to result in a high jump. Third, the right leg position in the air is essential for producing the force sufficient to create a fast sit spin after the landing. Finally, all of the preparatory and take-off motions are designed to enable the skater to take off and land without traveling a great distance across the ice.

The Flying Sit Spin

A

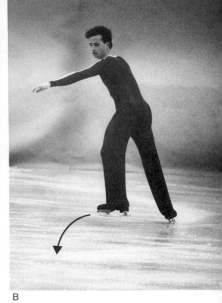

B

G

H

I

The best way to approach a flying sit spin is from back crossovers. The preparation edge for the spin requires strong clockwise rotation (A). As you shift your weight to the left forward outside take-off edge, step out of the preparation-edge circle (B). Allow your right leg to trail behind and across the left forward outside edge (C). Move your arms back and bend your left leg deeply (D). To lift off, swing your free leg around and your arms forward (E). Reach forward as you leave the ice (F). Tuck the left leg under you, leaving the right leg to the side. Then reach down with the left leg (G) to prepare for the landing and spin (H, I, J, K).

C
D
E
F

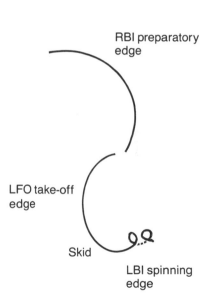

J
K

RBI preparatory
edge

LFO take-off
edge

Skid

LBI spinning
edge

**Preparation and take-off
edges for the flying sit spin.**
The preparation and take-off
edges for the flying sit spin
leave a reverse "S" imprint on
the ice.

Common Errors When Performing the Flying Sit Spin

A basic forward sit spin that is not centered is caused by:

- landing movements that are too slow or poorly timed;
- a take-off and landing that are not in nearly the same spot on the ice;
- the right leg not remaining to the side in the air;
- an insufficiently tight mirror-image "S" curve on the preparation and take-off edges;
- the right leg not passing around on the take-off edge.

A low jump is caused by:

- poor timing on the lift-off;
- inadequate use of the arms on the take-off;
- inadequate scrape on the take-off edge, precluding a pole-vaulting action. (A pole-vaulting action is essential on most jumps and is explained in detail in the chapter on jumps.)

A take-off edge that is clean is caused by:

- the right leg not passing around on the take-off edge;
- an insufficiently tight mirror-image "S" curve on the preparatory and take-off edges.

THE FLYING REVERSE SIT SPIN

In all respects until the take-off, the flying reverse sit spin is the same as the flying sit spin. The differences are a change of leg position in the air and a landing on a right back outside edge in a basic sit spin. Consequently, it should not be difficult to learn the flying reverse sit spin after having learned the flying sit spin.

As you take off, the only real difference is that you allow your right leg to come in front. The right leg position in the air will mimic its placement on a basic forward sit spin. Immediately after the left knee lifts up and you have tucked the left foot under your seat, switch leg positions: Your right leg comes into the tuck position and your left leg comes out in front. Once this leg switch is accomplished, the right leg should straighten in preparation for touchdown. As you can imagine, all of these movements must be done quite quickly since the time in the air is short. This is the principal challenge in the flying reverse sit spin.

As you land on a right back outside edge, proceed immediately into a basic back sit spin, using the arm motions described for the flying sit spin. The free (left) leg should already be in the spinning position.

Common Errors When Performing
the Flying Reverse Sit Spin

The primary difficulty in this maneuver is not reversing the leg positions quickly enough. This is caused by:

- leaving the right leg out to the side as you spring into the air;
- not tucking the left leg under immediately after the take-off;
- simply not executing a high enough jump to accomplish all of the movements.

In addition, you may find yourself spinning too slowly on the landing or not spinning in one place. This is caused by:

- proceeding too slowly into the basic back sit spin;
- making one of the centering errors described for the flying sit spin (see page 168).

THE FLYING CAMEL SIT SPIN,
OR DEATH DROP

The flying camel sit spin (also sometimes known as a flying open Axel sit spin) consists of a take-off from a left forward outside edge, going horizontal to the ice, stomach down, in the air, and landing on a right back outside edge in a basic back sit spin. A dramatic spin to say the least. Many a great skater has executed this move brilliantly. I was always proud of mine!

The preparation, preparatory edge, and the first part of the take-off edge are the same as those employed for the flying sit spin. As you approach the lift-off from the left forward outside edge, the technique and sensation change.

The Take-Off:
The free leg is allowed to swing around to a higher position on the lift-off and turns in slightly (although you will probably not notice the foot turning in, since it happens over a very short time). In fact, the right leg actually reaches up, into the air. The arms come forward but end up out to the side as lift-off occurs. The upper body rotates farther in the counterclockwise direction at lift-off than it does on the flying sit spin. There is a noticeable tendency to lean into the circle created by the take-off edge.

In essence, the take-off is a combination of take-offs for the flying camel spin and the flying sit spin, with decidedly more influence from the flying sit spin. You should even skid on the take-off edge, unlike the take-off edge on a

The Flying Camel Sit Spin, or Death Drop

A

B

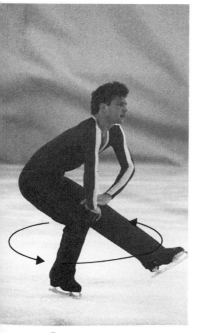

F

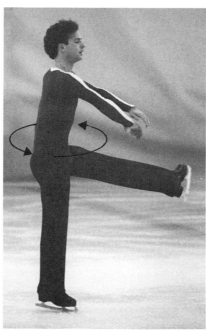

G

H

C

D

E

On the take-off for a death drop, the right leg should lift forward, high into the air (A). In the air, the legs are extended in opposite directions (B) and the body assumes a position horizontal to the ice. To prepare for the landing, reach for the ice with the right leg (C). On the landing, bend deeply at the waist (D) and flip over into a sit-spin position (E). To rise out of the spin, straighten your right leg (F). Keeping your free leg extended, straighten your back and raise your arms (G). Assume the standard exit position (H).

flying camel. The skid will create the pole-vaulting action needed to achieve considerable height on this flying spin.

The Jump:

As you spring into the air, your right leg will guide your lower body into the horizontal position. Your free leg exerts two forces: upward and backward. You welcome the upward force. The backward force, however, will tend to throw you off balance. To counteract this, arch your back and raise your chin as you lift into the air. This motion should not be so powerful that it prevents you from achieving a body position horizontal to the ice.

The right leg, as the leading force into the air, will reach its peak a split second before you reach the horizontal body position. Once it reaches its peak, gravity will exert a greater force on the right leg than will the slowly decreasing upward force of the body, causing the right leg to begin dropping toward the ice. The change in forces will initiate the preparation for touchdown. At the peak of the jump, when you are horizontal to the ice, you should begin to assist gravity by pushing your right foot down toward the ice. The left leg, which has lagged behind the right leg motion since the take-off, never quite catches up to the right leg and remains in the air during the touchdown preparation.

The entire motion in the air resembles both rolling over a barrel and scissoring the legs. These movements take place as you rotate nearly one and one-half revolutions in the air. It sounds quite complicated, but in practice it is rather straightforward.

The Landing:

Once your right foot touches the ice, you must execute a movement resembling the one used to enter the basic back sit spin—the "flip-over." As described for the basic back sit spin on page 150, the flip-over virtually eliminates body lean and positions the left hip for the back sit spin. When you land on a right back outside edge, your left leg will still be fairly high in the air—as far up as horizontal to the ice surface—and your hips will be square. In fact, your left hip and leg may be turned in slightly, since you will be leaning to the right. From this open position, execute the "flip-over" by turning out your left hip and leg while reducing the lean to the right.

As the "flip-over" comes to an end, move quickly into the basic back sit spin position, as you did on the flying reverse sit spin. Avoid the very common error of touching the ice with your left foot to help stabilize yourself for the back sit spin. You will end essentially in a back sit spin, the right back outside edge producing a series of tiny circles in one spot on the ice from the moment 173

of touchdown. Therefore, the point of take-off and the point of touchdown
should occur virtually on the same spot on the ice.

Common Errors When Performing
the Flying Camel Sit Spin

Difficulty in centering the back sit spin after the landing is caused by:

- not accomplishing the flip-over quickly enough;
- leaving the left leg out to the side while doing the flip-over;
- not keeping the back arched on the landing;
- not landing on the ball of the foot on a right back outside edge;
- not reaching early enough with the right leg for the landing.

Not reaching a horizontal position in the air is caused by:

- lack of scissoring action by the legs while in the air;
- not arching the back in the air;
- not keeping the chin up on the take-off and in the air;
- not reaching wide and high enough with the right leg—that is, not leading with the right leg into the air;
- insufficient height on the jump;
- poor timing on the take-off.

Insufficient height on the jump is caused by:

- lack of spring on the take-off;
- poor timing of the arms and free leg motion and the spring on the take-off;
- a clean take-off edge, or the opposite—too much shoulder and hip rotation on the take-off.

A clean take-off edge is caused by:

- an insufficiently wide swing of the free leg on the take-off;
- reverse "S" curve preparation and take-off edges that are insufficiently tight;
- incorrect timing of the rotation by the arms and shoulders on the preparation and take-off edges.

THE BUTTERFLY

The butterfly is aptly named since "butterfly" describes the position in the air of this flying spin. It consists of a take-off from two feet, a body position horizontal to the ice (similar to the position in a flying camel sit spin), and a landing in a back spin. In competition, the butterfly is commonly executed near the end of a skater's program since it does not require a great deal of energy or precision but does add to the technical content of a program.

The Preparation:

To prepare for a butterfly, do a right forward inside Mohawk, counterclockwise. After the Mohawk, skate on two feet. You will be on a right back outside edge and a left back inside edge. Your left arm should be in front and the right arm back. Without lingering in this position, dip the left shoulder down by pulling down with the left elbow. This will force you to lean forward. Keep your back arched. At the same time, look back over your left shoulder. Most of your weight should now be on your right foot, and your feet should be two to three feet apart, with your left leg out to the side.

The Take-Off:

To execute the lift-off, straighten your knees slightly and turn forward by doing a left back inside three-turn and a right outside back three-turn. During the turns, begin to shift your weight to the left foot. Immediately after the three-turns, bend your knees deeply and dip your left elbow and shoulder more. Begin to pass your left arm in an arc down toward the ice, then out to the side. Lift your right arm to the side in synchrony with your left arm. This should resemble the movement of a butterfly's wings as they move upward. Kick your right leg back and to the side as you spring from the left leg. Arch your back and lift your head even more than during the preparation.

Once in the air, your legs will scissor as they did in the flying camel sit spin. Hold your arms out to the side and keep your back arched as your legs execute a scissoring motion. Try to keep your legs apart during this movement. The scissor action will bring your left leg up and your right leg down, in anticipation of the landing.

The Landing:

The two constant features of the landing are that the right leg touches down first and that you are spinning. From this point, the skater can choose whether to do a back sit spin or a back upright spin, or, indeed, whether to prepare to

take off immediately into a second butterfly. An important issue is the achieve-
ment of sufficient height to lie horizontally in the air and to land gracefully and
gently. The technique on the preparation and take-off will determine whether
or not this is accomplished.

The one hurdle for a skater in learning the butterfly is the timing of the
take-off. The relationships between the weight shift and the windup, the upper
body movement and the lift-off, the spring and the butterfly motion are critical
to a successful butterfly. Timing, not technique, is the challenge.

12

Combination Spins

The flying spins and the basic spins can be combined in any number of sequences. The most important principle governing all of these combinations is the maintenance, or ideally the acceleration, of the rotational momentum that is created on the entrance into the first of a series of spins. This requires quick movements on the transitions. The transitions all consist of wide motions of the free leg and arms, which will ideally move from an open to a closed position. In addition, when a change of feet is required, the new center of rotation should be as close to the old as possible; in other words, don't step away from the center of the first spin. If you follow this fundamental principle of maintaining/accelerating rotational momentum, combination spins are no more difficult than basic or flying spins.

Since there are far too many possible combinations to discuss here, I shall describe only the techniques for common transitions and for unusual combinations that require special consideration, all in the counterclockwise direction. From this discussion, you will be able to translate the techniques of any number of combinations.

Two types of transitions will be discussed: transitions involving a change of feet and changes in position on one foot.

TRANSITIONS ON TWO FEET

A Forward Upright Spin
Into a Back Upright Spin

The object of this transition is to follow one very fast spin with another. This means that the fast-forward upright spin must be completed before changing feet for the fast-back upright spin.

Spin combinations require quick movement during the transition from one spin to the next. Here, Olympic Gold Medalist Katarina Witt performs a layback spin as part of a spin combination.

Upon completion of the fast-forward upright spin, uncross your right foot and place it on the ice next to the left foot, toe to toe. Open your arms to the side and bend your left leg slightly. Turn your head from a position over your left shoulder to a position looking straight ahead.

As you begin to shift your weight to the right back outside edge, execute a left back push-off just as you would for a push-off onto an ordinary right back outside edge. At the end of the push-off, straighten your right knee and lift your left foot while turning your left hip outward. Place your left leg in the position appropriate for the beginning of a fast-back upright spin, then execute that spin.

A Back Upright Spin
Into a Forward Upright Spin

The object of this transition is the same as the preceding one: to accomplish two fast spins, back-to-back.

At the completion of a fast-back upright spin, uncross your left foot and place it on a forward outside edge next to your right foot. Bend your knees and open your arms out to the side. Face straight ahead.

Immediately transfer your weight to the left foot by pushing with the right foot. The push-off consists of a thrust against the ice with the heel of the right foot on a forward inside edge. The edge should create an imprint on the ice that has an increasingly large arc. As the push evolves, bend your left knee.

At the end of the push-off, lift your right foot off the ice and turn a left forward outside three-turn. You now will be spinning on a left back inside edge. Bring your right leg in front as you would for the basic fast-forward upright spin, and straighten your left leg. Execute a fast-forward upright spin.

The most common error during this transition occurs on the change of feet. You will be tempted to step away from the center of the fast-back upright spin, but you should avoid that at all costs. Ideally you will use the same center for the forward upright spin as you did for the fast-back spin. This means that the step onto the left foot should be merely a change of feet and that the power for the second spin comes almost entirely from the circular push-off with the right foot. It also means that you must lead with the left arm and shoulder during the transition by pressing them backward.

A Basic Forward Sit Spin
Into a Basic Back Sit Spin

The transition from the basic forward sit spin position into the basic back sit spin position should be accomplished without rising up off the knee (rising up off the knee is a very common mistake). The top of your head should remain at a constant distance from the ice.

The first part of the transition consists of all the movements through switching the feet. You execute these movements simultaneously, while keeping your back arched and chin up: Bring your right foot next to your left foot and turn the right toe in. Open your arms out to the side. Place your right foot on a back outside edge and push out to the side with your left leg. The left leg motion resembles a push-off onto a right back outside edge but is more difficult and awkward since your right leg is bent in a back sit spin position. At the end of the push, the left leg should be fully extended out to the side with the blade on a back inside edge, skating a circle. However, once the leg is extended, your foot should not remain on the ice.

The second part of the transition is aimed at resuming the rotational speed on the spin and, therefore, must be done rapidly. Bring your arms into the position for a basic back sit spin. Flip your left leg over—that is, turn it out at the hip—so that it comes into the basic back sit spin position. Since you are spinning, you will rotate to meet the left leg as you turn it out. Ideally, the transition should not take more time than it takes to complete one full rotation. This means that you must execute the movements relatively rapidly. Remember, don't come up in the knees as you do the transition. This will cause you to lose your balance and will slow the spin.

A Basic Back Sit Spin
Into a Basic Forward Sit Spin

This transition can also be thought of as having two parts. The first part consists of changing feet and preparing for the acceleration of the rotational momentum. Bring your left foot next to your right foot. Open your arms out to the side. Shift your weight to the left forward outside edge while pushing out to the side with your right foot, which will be on a forward inside edge. This will be easier if you push with the back part of the right blade.

Once your right leg is fully extended, the second part of the transition begins. Swing your right leg around into the position for a basic forward sit spin and bring your arms into the closed sit spin position. This will produce a left forward outside three-turn. The turn places you on the correct edge for the spin—a left back inside edge.

As in the case of the transition from the basic forward sit spin into a basic back sit spin, you must keep your knees bent. Also, the movements should be executed quite strongly and rapidly.

A Basic Forward Camel Spin
Into a Basic Back Camel Spin

During the transition, it is important to maintain the camel position in the upper body. This means that your body remains horizontal to the ice and your back is arched. The knees, however, will bend to accomplish the push-off into the back camel spin.

Swing your right leg around and down in a wide arc so that the right foot ends up next to the left foot. Turn the right toe in in preparation for the weight shift to the right back outside edge. Bend both knees. As you shift your weight to the right back outside edge, push off with your left foot as you would onto a right back outside edge. At the end of the push, your left leg should be out to the side. From that point, you must lift it and swing it around and back into the basic back camel position. This movement should be continuous from the beginning of the push-off to the back camel position.

The key to this transition is the wide swing of each leg on the first and second halves of the transition movement. The wider the arc, the faster the back camel spin after the transition.

A Basic Back Camel Spin
Into a Basic Forward Camel Spin

This transition requires a more dramatic change in body position and can also be divided into two segments. During the first segment, straighten your body up from the camel position and bring your left leg down. Place your left foot next to your right foot in preparation for the weight shift. Your arms remain basically out to the side, although the left arm and shoulder should be slightly in front.

The second part of the transition begins with the shift of weight to a left forward outside edge. Simultaneously push from a right forward inside edge. This thrusting motion should create a curved inside edge that increases in radius as it progresses. Bend your left leg deeply during the push-off.

Once the right leg is fully extended, execute a left forward outside three-turn so that you are now spinning on a left back inside edge—the proper edge for a basic forward camel spin. Lean forward, arch the back, and lift the right leg behind for the camel spin position. Lead with the left arm and shoulder, which are pulling the body and which are moving counterclockwise. Straighten the left leg.

Speed on the basic forward camel spin is dependent upon the arc of the right foot's push-off, the speed of the push-off, and the relative timing of the

Debi Thomas displays perfect technique on the back camel: chin up, arms and free leg fully extended, and the knee of the skating leg locked. Also, the spin is precisely centered.

lift over the left leg, the push-off, and the pull with the left arm. In the first instance, the arc of the push-off should be as wide as possible. In the matter of timing, it is important that all these movements occur simultaneously and reach their end points at the same time.

Camel Spins Into Sit Spins

For the first half of the transition, a forward camel spin into a back sit spin utilizes basically the same techniques as those for the transition from a forward camel spin into a back camel spin. In fact, the only significant difference is that you assume an upright body position as your right foot moves next to the left foot in preparation for the weight change. The technique for the second half of the transition is the same as that used for the forward into the back sit spin. Obviously, as you shift your weight to the right foot and push with the left leg, you will bend your right leg in order to assume a sit spin position. At the end of the push-off, the left leg will fall in front into the sit spin position.

In the case of a transition from a back camel spin into a forward sit spin, the technique for the first half of the transition is identical to that employed in the transition from a back camel spin into a forward camel spin. The second half of the transition is the same as that use for the back into the forward sit spin, with one exception: As you push off, you bend your left leg and bring your right leg in front into the standard sit spin position.

Sit Spin Into Camel Spin

To move from a forward sit spin into a back camel spin, you must partially straighten your left leg before beginning to shift your weight to the right foot. It is important not to straighten your left knee too much. If you do, you won't have enough power to accomplish a successful push-off. The remainder of the transition is the same as that used for a forward-into-back camel spin. The movements throughout the transition should be continuous, smooth, and rapid, with the arms and legs moving in a wide arc around the body.

To make the transition from a back sit spin into a forward camel spin, come up on the right knee as described above. As you do, bring your left foot next to your right foot, and turn a right back outside three-turn in preparation for the push-off into the forward camel. The second half of the transition is identical to the back-into-forward camel spin. Throughout these movements, lean forward, but keep your head arched.

TRANSITIONS ON ONE FOOT

A transition from one spin position into another on the same foot is more difficult in many respects than a transition involving a change of feet. Maximizing rotational momentum is difficult and requires great skill. In some cases, it is impossible to increase the speed of the spin on the second position: all you can hope for is to maintain your speed. In nearly all cases, speed on the second spin is dependent on the movement of the free leg and the arms. Balance is critical as the transition is executed.

A Forward Sit Spin Into a Forward Camel Spin

This transition is not frequently used, although it has a certain beauty. It is virtually impossible to accelerate the speed of the spin as you transit into the camel spin. Therefore, the most important feature is maintaining balance and giving the impression of perfect control as the transition proceeds.

From the sit spin position, begin to slowly straighten your left leg. Do not straighten your body; rather, move directly from the sit-spin position into the camel position without standing straight. As you change position, bring your right foot toward your left foot, turning your right hip in as you do. When your right foot reaches your left foot, your upper body should be halfway to the camel position. By this time your arms should be out to the side.

Continue to rise over the left leg, and pass your right leg behind, into the camel position. The path of movement for the right leg should carry it slightly across and behind the left leg. Turning your right foot in as you do this—slightly pigeon-toed—will help you keep your balance by forcing you to remain on a left back inside edge. (Don't forget to turn the right foot and hip out once in the camel position.)

Throughout this movement, it is important to keep your back arched and your chin up. Also, it should feel as though you are looking back over your left shoulder and that your body is twisted slightly to the left, even though the upper body is horizontal to the ice. This will counterbalance the pigeon-toed position of the right foot and the lean inherent in the left back inside edge. Remember to remain on the ball of the foot as you make the transition.

A Back Sit Spin
Into a Back Camel Spin

This transition does permit the skater to maintain the speed of the back sit spin, at the very least, and with perfect technique, to increase the speed slightly upon entering the back camel spin. The speed is created totally by the movement of the left arm and leg, as a result of the wide arc through which they pass. This means that the free leg and arm must move around faster than the speed of the spin, for two reasons: 1) they are going in the same direction as the spin and must pass from a position trailing the body to one leading the body; and 2) they are moving in a wide arc, requiring faster speed since they constitute the part of the body that is the farthest from the center of the rotation.

From the back sit spin, begin to straighten your right leg. As you do this, bring your left leg around to the back on a wide arc. This final position of the left leg, obviously, is the back camel position. Also, move your left arm, which has been in a sit spin position, in an arc similar to that of the left leg. The right arm is passive and can remain down. Simultaneous to the left leg and arm movements, allow your upper body to lean forward into the camel position, keeping your chin up and your back arched. Remain on the ball of the foot throughout the transition.

Maintaining rotational speed depends on the free leg and arm creating a wide arc, and on the synchronization of these movements with the rise into the camel position. Balance and smoothness are critical elements of a successful transition.

A Forward Camel Spin
Into a Forward Sit Spin

This transition can actually create a fast sit spin. Three reasons account for the increase in rotational momentum. First, the camel spin consists of a relatively open position. Contracting this into the relatively closed sit spin position produces additional rotational momentum. Second, the camel position is up, whereas the sit spin position is down. (You will recall that moving the body closer to the point of rotation, the place where the rotating body and the stationary earth meet, creates rotational momentum.) Third, the free leg moves from an open position in back through a wide arc into a closed position in front. The weight of the leg moving faster than the speed of the spin leads the body into faster rotation. (The free leg must move faster than the body because it is farther from the center of rotation and because it must move in the same direction from behind to a position in front of the body.) Provided that balance is maintained, with the weight securely on the ball of the foot, all of these factors will contribute to a fast spin.

To create speed, you must execute the transition fairly rapidly. From the camel spin position, swing your right leg in a wide arc from behind to the sit spin position in front. Simultaneously bend your left leg into a sit spin position. Keep your back arched, your chin up, and remain on a left back inside edge throughout the transition. You will discover that this one-foot change of position is the easiest of all the transitions and can be great fun.

A Back Camel Spin
Into a Back Sit Spin

Even though you are moving from an open to a closed position, it is slightly more difficult to create speed on this one-foot position change than on the preceding one. This is because the free leg moves more slowly than the body as it passes from a camel spin position behind the body to a sit spin position in front. In other words, the body must catch up with the free leg, and therefore the free leg merely folds in front of the body. The only motion contributing to additional rotational momentum is the contraction of the open position into the closed position.

The transition from a back camel into a back sit spin begins by bending the right leg. As this occurs, place your arms out to the side. While remaining on the ball of the skate, "flip over" the left hip in a manner similar to that which you used to complete the jump on the flying camel sit spin. This "flip-over" essentially involves turning out the left hip as the body moves to a more upright position, and as the right leg bends into a sit spin position. Bring your arms into the contracted sit spin position and allow the free leg to fold in front of you. And yet another reminder: Keep your back arched and your chin up.

The Hamill Camel

The Hamill camel was made famous by Dorothy Hamill, the 1976 World and Olympic Champion. While Dorothy was a strong, athletic, yet graceful skater who is remembered for her wonderful personality as well as her skating ability, she will always be identified with the Hamill camel.

Dorothy Hamill during her gold-medal-winning performance at the 1976 Olympic Games.

The technique, while exacting, is fairly straightforward. From a back camel spin, bend your right leg into a sit spin position. Your back will inevitably collapse slightly from its previously arched position—it will hunch over. Try to keep your free leg as high as possible, but realize that it also will tend to droop slightly.

From this position close to the ice, "flip over" your left hip by turning the left leg and hip out and bringing your body up and into a sit spin position. Avoid the common error of touching the ice with your left foot as you do this. You should now be in a solid back sit spin.

OTHER TRANSITIONS

There are many other spin combinations that require transitions. However, most of these demand techniques virtually identical to those just described. The only differences will relate to adapting the upper body from the original position to the position used in the second spin. For example, a back camel spin into a fast-forward upright spin uses similar techniques to those employed to make the transition from the back camel spin into the forward sit spin. The differences are that you do not go down into a sit spin position during the push into the second part of the spin, and your right leg ends up in a slightly different position (as do your arms)—a position for a forward upright spin.

A few unusual combinations do require special techniques.

The Back Camel Jump Sit Spin

The back camel jump sit spin involves a back camel spin with a jump into a forward sit spin. This transition is, in reality, a flying spin in which the jump is in the middle of the spin and results in a change of feet and of position. Although this maneuver sounds relatively straightforward, it is difficult to do well and involves some complicated techniques.

You can break down the back camel jump sit spin into three segments: 1) the preparation, 2) the jump, and 3) the landing.

The Preparation:

The preparation for the jump is rather unusual, due to the position from which you will jump, that is, a camel position. From a back camel spin, bend your right leg in preparation for the spring. As you bend your knee, push your left shoulder toward the ice and lower your left arm. This downward pressure on the left side of your body will tend to cause your back to hunch. Do not let this occur. Continue to arch your back and keep your chin up strongly. Also do not let your free leg drop.

The Jump:
The next segment involves the spring into the jump. The jump is essentially a "flip-over." Throw your left arm to the side into a wide vertical arc. Follow with the right arm coming across the front of your body. This will cause your upper body to feel as if you are facing upward with your back toward the ice, horizontally. While you will be leaning back, you will not actually be horizontal to the ice but in fact will be more upright. Simultaneously, spring from the right leg.

As you leave the ice, you will feel as if you are jumping over your left hip. This will cause the left leg to drop in preparation for the landing. As this occurs, place your right leg out to the side, as far away as possible. In the middle of the jump, your body will move into an upright position.

The force on the jump ("flip-over") should be sufficient to create a full revolution in the air. You will be jumping from a right back outside edge onto a left back inside edge. This is actually less demanding than it sounds.

The Landing:
When you land, your weight should be on the ball of your left foot. The landing employs the same techniques as those that were used on the landing for the flying sit spin. Contract quickly into the sit spin position by bringing your free leg around to the front, by closing your arms into the sit spin position, and by bending your left leg. The contraction should occur as soon as you touch down.

The "Flipover" for a Back Camel
Into a Forward Sit Spin

A

B

C

G

H

The "flipover" for a back camel (A) into a forward sit spin requires that you lean back as you jump over the left hip (B). In the air, you will feel as though you are leaning back, horizontal to the ice (C). Note, as he lands the flipover (D, E), how Brian Boitano quickly reaches down to grasp his right leg with his right hand, while simultaneously bending deeply at the left knee (F, G, H).

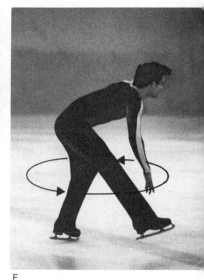

D   E   F

The Back Sit Spin
Jump Forward Sit Spin

The technique for this maneuver is virtually the same as that for the back camel jump sit spin, except for the fact that you start from a sit spin position. You spring from a back sit spin into an open position in the air—arms out to the sides, left leg reaching forward, and right leg reaching to the side. The technique for the remainder of the move is the same.

The Forward Camel Spin
Jump Back Sit Spin

This transition requires that you pass through a forward upright spin for a split second in preparation for the jump. As you come out of the forward camel spin, open your arms out to the side, bring your body upright, and swing your free leg on a wide arc around the left leg. It should almost feel as though the leg is swinging around in front of you. As it swings around, bend your left leg.

  As the free leg is coming in front, spring into the air. After rotating half a revolution, land on a right back outside edge and contract into a sit spin. The success of this maneuver depends on the wide passage of the free leg and the timing of the lift-off.

Whatever combination of spins you choose to attempt, quickness, control, and strength are the keys to performing them successfully.

The Forward Sit Spin
Jump Back Sit Spin

Since the free leg is already in front on the forward sit spin, all you must do on this maneuver is spring from the forward sit spin. Once in the air, change your foot position so that your right leg is down toward the ice and your left leg is in front. Land on a right back outside edge, and then contract immediately into a back sit spin. The key to this transition is springing directly from the forward sit spin position.

13

Jumps: General Principles and Positions

There are a number of factors that pertain to all jumps and that dictate the technique required for excellent jumping. Before embarking on a discussion of the individual jumps, it's important to understand the general physical principles that govern jumping.

As previously mentioned, the principles of angular momentum govern figure skating. While jumping into the air from dry land is fundamentally a linear action, jumping on ice is complicated by the many forces that create angular momentum. Nearly all jumps in figure skating involve rotation. Therefore a jump on ice is more complex than a jump on dry land. There are simply many more forces to be aware of and to control.

It is essential to recognize that the tendency of an edge is toward the center of the circle created by that edge. You can observe this by rolling a coin on its edge and watching the result. In addition, the upper body, the arms, and the free leg have a tendency to be pulled along by the force of the edge. In fact, the arms, free leg, and upper body, if allowed to follow passively, will eventually overtake the rotational force of the edge and will rotate faster. We have effectively employed this principle to create faster spins. Both the inherent force of the edge and the force generated by the arms, upper body, and free leg tend to increase rotation. Successful jumping requires the precise control of these two forces.

The degree of curvature of an edge is determined by the lean of the body. Once this lean is established, you must live with the edge as it is and with the resulting inherent angular momentum. Lean is the mechanism by which you regulate the inherent angular momentum of the edge.

The upper body, arms, and free leg are controlled by the checks on the preparation and take-off. These are designed to produce the correct amount of

193

Excellent jumping combines athleticism and grace.

rotation on the take-off. Too much rotation will result in the upper body overtaking the edge and precluding maximum lift. Too little rotation means that you will be fighting the edge and will not arrive at the correct position for the take-off.

This may sound obvious and simple—and it is. What makes it complex is that you, the skater, must keep track of the many different movements and positions of different parts of your body and the timing of those movements relative to each other and to the jump. This is why competitive skaters practice for many hours a day. Controlling all these movements and forces is a challenge. Once learned, though, it becomes second nature.

One other point is worth noting. To jump, you must spring off the ice. To do this, you must be strong and quick. The lift-off requires a very rapid thrust, and the development of quick muscular reactions is essential. Most training centers have instructors who can teach off-ice exercises designed to achieve muscular strength and quickness. In addition, being able to stroke rapidly on the ice is helpful.

There are two types of jumps: edge jumps and toe jumps. Edge jumps involve a take-off from one foot, while toe jumps require both feet on the ice for the take-off. For reasons I shall describe for each jump, toe jumps are not necessarily easier in terms of controlling rotation on the take-off.

THE BASIC POSITION IN THE AIR

Once in the air, all basic rotational jumps have one common position. That position, for counterclockwise jumps (as with spins, the only direction I will describe in detail), consists of the following:

- the left leg crossed over the right, with the feet together and the legs comfortably straight;
- the hands clenched in front of the chest, with the elbows down and about four to six inches from the body, in a prayer-like position (the elbows being used for balance); and
- the head facing over the left shoulder.

This position is best learned in the context of a loop jump, which I shall describe in Chapter 14. This body position applies only to the basic rotational jumps. Some jumps, described later, require different positions. There are several common errors in jumping to watch out for.

1. Many skaters have a tendency to lift their shoulders on the take-off.
This dissipates some of the upward force and results in a lower jump. It can also disturb your balance.

2. Sometimes skaters find it difficult to cross their feet in the air. This will slow down the rotation and will make it more difficult to land the jump. When you are having trouble completing the required number of revolutions on a particular jump, the first place to look is at the feet—are they crossed tightly in the air?

3. Occasionally skaters will cross their legs but will allow the left foot to lift toward the right knee. This is called a "wrap" and can fatally impair consistency on jumps. A "wrap" can also occur when the legs are too far apart, even though they are crossed.

4. If you do not look over your left shoulder, the rotation in the air will not reach its maximum speed.

5. Any deviation from a straight body position with an arched back will disturb the balance and can preclude a successful landing. The body must be absolutely straight in the air.

LANDING

The landing is the same for most basic rotational jumps: a right back outside edge. Before you actually touch down, it is important to prepare for the landing as you approach the ice. The first step is to slow the rotation, which you accomplish by beginning to open your arms out to the side and allowing your head to face forward. These two actions will slow the rotation and will allow your legs to prepare for the landing. As the rotation slows, reach for the ice with your right foot, allowing your left leg to bend slightly at the knee and your left foot to move slightly away from the right leg, toward the middle of the right shin. All of these movements occur in the span of a split second. On average, the time spent in the air is about one second. As high as I jumped, I never spent more than two and a half seconds in the air.

The first part of your body to touch the ice will be the ball of your right foot. From this point on, the landing uses the same technique that you have (faithfully!) practiced for the exit from the fast-back upright spin. Once touch-down has occurred, bend your right leg immediately to cushion the landing, and proceed with the exit. The quicker you are in executing the exit, or in this case, the landing position, the better are your chances of landing the jump successfully. In fact, after the take-off, the actual landing is the most critical factor influencing whether you will execute the jump successfully.

Common rotating and landing positions for the jumps.
The common rotating position in the air during a jump consists of the left leg crossed over the right, the arms in a prayer-like position, and the head turned over the left shoulder (A). To land, open the arms and legs, reach down with the right foot, and look to the right (B). Bend the right knee deeply as you hit the ice, and hold the landing position for a count of five (C).

A

I have described the position in the air for basic rotational jumps consisting of one or more rotations. As revolutions are added, that position must become tighter and the check position on the landing stronger. Similarly, the higher you jump, the more time you have to execute these actions but the deeper the bend in the right knee must be to cushion the landing properly.

Two variations on landings for rotational jumps are worth noting. The first is a landing on a left back inside edge. This is frequently employed in the context of jump combinations. The principles pertaining to landing on a right back outside edge pertain here as well. The only differences are that the crossed free foot is not unraveled prior to the landing and, following touchdown, the arms and shoulders should be parallel with the skating foot, with the right arm back and the free leg extended straight back, without being turned out.

Edge jumps landed on a left back inside edge are referred to as half jumps (such as the half loop), with one exception: the Axel is called a one-foot Axel (invented by Ernst Oppacher of Austria). Likewise, toe jumps landed on a left back inside edge are called one-foot jumps.

The second variation is a toe-assisted forward landing. Skaters frequently use this method for toe jumps in the midst of a jump combination. You can choose to land on a right forward inside edge with a left toe assist, or a left forward outside edge with a right toe assist. The former is somewhat more difficult since it means unraveling the legs prior to touchdown. Toe jumps employing such a landing are referred to as half jumps—for example, the half flip.

B

C

Preparation for a left back inside edge landing.

On the preparation for a left back inside edge landing, open your arms and lift your right foot behind you (A). Check the rotation on the landing by extending the right leg (B).

A

B

14

Edge Jumps

Edge jumps require precise rotational control of the upper body, arms, and free leg, and of the lean on the take-off edge. To achieve a good jump, the checks on the preparation and take-off must be perfectly timed. All edge jumps, with two exceptions, involve rotating in the air in the same direction as the inherent rotation of the take-off edge. (The two exceptions are the bunny hop, which involves a take-off from the flat of the blade, and the Walley, in which the rotation in the air is the opposite of the rotation of the edge.) Therefore, controlling the rotation on the preparation and take-off will be one of the most important considerations.

THE BUNNY HOP

The bunny hop, which consists of a forward take-off from the left foot and a forward landing on the right toe pick and the left foot, will more than likely be the first jump you learn. This is because it is the only jump in skating that involves linear momentum. In other words, there is no rotation, since the take-off is from the flat of the blade, not from an edge. In addition, it will prepare you for the waltz jump, which is the next jump you will learn.

To gain speed for the jump, stroke forward in a straight line. For the immediate preparation, place all your weight on your right foot. You should be skating in a straight line, meaning that you are on the flat of the blade. Your left arm is in front, and your right arm is to the side. Your body should be upright, with your back arched, your chin up, and your head facing straight ahead.

Step onto the left foot for the take-off. Again, you will be on the flat of the

199

Edge jumps require precise rotational control,
particularly during the preparation and take-off.

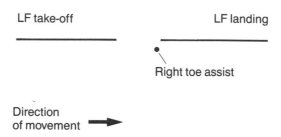

Pattern of the imprint on the ice created by the bunny hop.

blade. As you step, move your arms as if you were walking on dry land—the left arm passes back as you step forward with the left foot, and the right arm passes in front as the right leg passes back. As the arms move, they pass close to the body. (This motion will be repeated in the opposite direction on the take-off.) Extend the right leg back and bend the left leg.

It is now time to lift into the air on your first jump. The jump itself consists of several motions, all of which occur smoothly and simultaneously.

- Pass the free (right) leg in front on a straight path parallel to the left leg.
- Change your arm positions in an exaggerated walking fashion, so that they finish parallel to the ice.
- Spring from the left leg.
- Lean forward slightly as you spring.
- As you spring, the last thing to leave the ice is the toe pick of the left blade.
- Maintain the arm positions in the air.

In preparation for the landing, reach for the ice with your right foot, toe pick first. Once the right toe pick touches the ice, immediately place the left foot on the ice, skating on the flat of the blade. Essentially, you will be pushing onto your left foot, using the right toe pick for the thrust. Your right leg will therefore end up extended behind you. As you push off, move your arms in a walking fashion so that your right arm is now in front and your left arm is back and to the side.

To repeat the bunny hop, you can prepare again or, better yet, do another one from the landing of the first. The landing places you in the correct position for the take-off.

THE WALTZ JUMP

The waltz jump consists of a take-off from a left forward outside edge, half a revolution in the air, and a landing on a right back outside edge. While it is the simplest of the major jumps, the waltz jump can be one of the most beautiful—it is the only one in which the skater can virtually float in the air. This is possible because only half a revolution is required and the arms and legs are in an open position during the jump. In many respects, it is very similar to the grand jeté that is done in ballet. Regrettably, the waltz jump is rarely executed in the course of major competitions today. Perhaps when a skater comes along who can jump very high, the beauty of this jump will make it an enviable feature of his or her competitive routine.

The Preparation:

The most useful and common preparation is a right back outside edge. Before stepping onto the preparation edge, you can gain speed by doing back cross-overs in the counterclockwise direction or by skating forward into a counter-clockwise inside Mohawk.

On the preparation edge, hold your left arm and shoulder back while your right arm remains more or less in front. You want to look in the direction you are going—that is, over the left shoulder. This position will enable you to step onto the take-off edge without initiating any unnecessary rotational motion.

From this preparation edge through the completion of the jump, the lean of the body is critical; it must be toward the center of the circle inscribed by the skating edge. Remember to keep your hips under you. This is made easier if, on the step, you place the heel of your free foot against the heel of your skating foot, bending both knees. With your hips under you, you will stabilize your lean and get your weight directly over your skating foot.

Once in the preparatory edge position, hold it for a second or two so that all rotational movement in the upper body comes to a halt. This is one of those times when you must forsake fluidity for control.

The Transition:

The next stage is the transition from the preparatory edge to the take-off edge: a change from a right back outside edge to a left forward outside edge. You will find that when you change both feet and position at the same time, you can easily lose your balance. There are two precautionary actions that you can take to help maintain your balance through the transition.

1. Make the change from one foot to the other a "step," not a "push."
2. Just before the step, shift the weight on your right foot to the back of the blade. This will help to prevent your free foot from gliding across and behind the skating foot and will help to keep your lean toward the center of the circle. Tucking your hips under will also contribute to maintaining the proper lean.

When you step, move your torso forward, so that it is slightly ahead of the skating foot. It is useful to imagine that your left shoulder and your chin are leading the body. Your right shoulder should feel pressed back. This will enable you both to arch your back over your left hip and to lean forward, ahead of the skate. This forward lean will serve to counteract the backward force of your arms and free leg when they pass forward on the actual lift-off.

After you step onto the left foot, your left arm should be in front of you, your right arm slightly behind you, both pointing to the ice but not close to your body. Your right leg, now the free leg, should be extended back, close to the ice, straight but not locked. Your left leg, now the skating leg, should be bent as deeply as possible.

The Take-Off:

It's now time to start the movement that will take you into the air. The entire lift-off motion must be continuous—timing is critical. In the simplest of terms, the upward and outward thrust of your arms and legs must occur simultaneously, along with the pole-vault action of the skating toe spiking the ice on the take-off.

Move your arms in an elliptical pattern, passing them back, away from the body, then forward close to the body. Their final position is in front, spread apart slightly, at shoulder height.

Move your free leg forward. It should start in a position directly behind your free hip and pass through on a relatively straight path, held straight throughout the entire motion. It's rather like kicking a football. By keeping the free knee straight, you will increase the upward and outward force, making the jump higher.

When you first made the step, you bent your left leg. Now, as your arms move back, bend even more. The more you bend, the higher you'll jump. The spring occurs as your arms and free (right) leg pass forward.

Throughout the take-off, look straight ahead and keep your chin up. Thinking up and looking up will prepare you psychologically for the spring.

The last part of the skating foot to leave the ice is the toe pick. It serves the skater in the same way that the pole serves the pole vaulter.

The Float:

Once in the air, spread your arms slightly and keep them out for the entire jump. On the take-off, you passed your free leg forward, to a position in front of you and parallel to the ice. Now that you are in the air, it will fall naturally, pulled down by gravity. This will prepare it for the landing. As your right leg falls, lift your left leg slightly. This will give your jump the illusion of greater height.

The landing should be on the same circle that was created by the preparatory and take-off edges. As skating is rotational by nature, the half rotation you need to execute this jump successfully is not a problem. Use the standard landing position and check (see page 195).

The imprint made on the ice during take-off and landing is useful as a diagnostic tool for identifying errors in technique. Try to locate relatively clean ice for the execution of the waltz jump when you are first learning it or when you are experiencing difficulties. The spatial relationship between the preparatory and take-off edges, the integrity of the take-off edge itself, and the relationship between the take-off and landing edges can indicate whether or not you have employed the correct technique. This diagnostic approach will be particularly important when you are learning the next jump, the Axel.

The preparatory and take-off edges should form one continuous circle consisting of a gradual curve and, therefore, only a little lean into the circle. Ideally, the preparatory edge should be contiguous with the take-off edge. If the preparatory edge glides into the circle, the right leg will be in an incorrect position as the weight is shifted to the left foot. It will be across and behind, meaning that it must swing around as it passes to its position in front on the take-off. This will create excessive rotational momentum on the take-off, resulting in either a skid on the take-off edge or a "waxel" (see page 211).

Toward the end of the take-off edge, the edge will begin to curve a little more. Nevertheless, the edge should be clean—that is, without a skid. A skid indicates that the upper body or the hips have rotated too far and are pulling the lower body and skate around. At the end of the take-off edge, you should see a toe-pick mark, indicating that the toe pick has served as a pole vault.

G   F   E

Pattern followed on the preparation, take-off, and landing for a waltz jump.

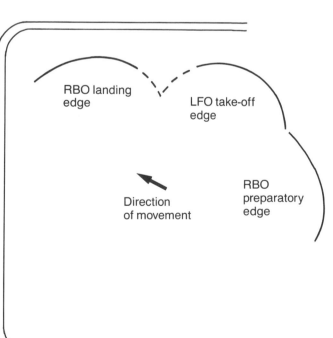

RBO landing edge

LFO take-off edge

RBO preparatory edge

End of rink

Direction of movement

D   C   B   A

The most common preparation edge for a waltz jump is a right back outside edge. You can gain speed going into the edge by doing back crossovers or by skating forward into an inside Mohawk. Once on the edge, hold it for a second or two to arrest all rotational movement in the upper body (A). On the step with the left foot, your weight must be directly over the left leg and the right leg should be directly behind the left. Keep your right shoulder back as you bend and extend your legs for the spring into the air (B). Reach forward with the arms and free leg as you lift from the left toe pick (C). Once in the air, let your arms and legs remain in the open position (D). Land, using the conventional landing technique described on page 195 (E, F, G).

THE AXEL

The Axel consists of a take-off from a left forward outside edge, a counterclockwise rotation of one and a half turns in the air, and a landing on a right back outside edge. In other words, the Axel is a waltz jump with an additional rotation in the air. It can also be described as a waltz jump combined with a loop jump. In fact, it is important to learn the loop after having conquered the waltz jump and before attempting the Axel (see page 224).

The Axel was invented by Axel Paulsen, a Norwegian skater who rose to international fame before the turn of the century. Paulsen performed the first Axel as a special figure in Vienna at the first known International-style competition, in 1882. Since its inception, the jump has undergone many technical and artistic changes; the technique today is better defined for consistency and excellence, and many variations have been added, enhancing the beauty of its execution. It is one of the most versatile of all jumps. In my opinion, there is no more exciting jump than a high, broad, floating delayed Axel. Yet it is one of the most difficult jumps, the one jump that requires almost infallible precision.

The Single Axel

For the ordinary Axel, the preparation and take-off technique are basically the same as those used for the waltz jump. The only significant difference is that you have to accomplish one more revolution. In the air, retract into the rotational position: your arms folded in a prayer-like fashion with the hands in front of the chest, your left leg crossed over the right, and your head over the left shoulder. Turning your head over your left shoulder will increase the speed of your rotations in the air. With the proper balance and arm technique, your legs will fall into the rotational position automatically. After about one revolution, it's time to start thinking about stopping the rotation. Release your arms and extend them outward in the check position, arms out to the side. Your left leg should lift slightly in preparation for the landing. Return your head to the straight forward position.

When you hit the ice, check hard by pressing your right shoulder slightly back and holding your left arm firmly at a 45-degree angle to your line of flight.

The Delayed Axel

Although an ordinary Axel has its place, there is a theory that the delayed Axel is the first type of Axel you should learn. A delayed jump is one in which the rotation at the beginning of the jump proceeds very slowly. (In fact, the speed of rotation is equal to the speed of rotation inherent on the take-off edge.) However, it requires a special kind of person—one with patience and the willingness to persevere. If you are that kind of person, then it's well worth the effort to learn the delayed Axel first.

The first thing to do is shed any fears you may have about completing the required one and a half revolutions. This is a needless worry and can be counterproductive. With the proper technique and timing, and just a bit of spring, you can easily accomplish the delay plus the revolutions.

As it turns out, there are only two differences between an ordinary Axel and a delayed Axel; it is really not as complicated as it sounds. First, during the take-off edge, focus your eyes on a spot straight ahead and about 20 feet above the ground. Don't take your eyes off this spot until you bring your arms into the rotational position. It's time to bring your arms in when it is no longer possible to look at the object—that is, when the shoulders have rotated to the point at which your head has begun to turn away from your point of focus. At this point, move your head into the rotational position. Second, while the head is "spotting" (focusing on that spot straight ahead), keep your arms in their final lift-off position, that is, in front of you at shoulder level. Coupled with the head spot, this will give you the chance to experience that unique and wonderful feeling of being suspended in air.

The preparation for the landing and the landing itself are basically the same as for the ordinary single Axel, except that the increased speed of the rotation in the air at the end of this jump requires a stronger check on landing.

E   D   C

On a delayed Axel, focus on a spot straight ahead and about 20 feet above the ground as you perform the take-off (A, B). When you can no longer focus on the spot—that is, when your shoulders have rotated to the point at which your head has begun to turn away from the point of focus—retract your arms and legs into the rotating position and look over your left shoulder (C,D). With the proper technique and timing, you'll be able to complete the Axel's one and a half rotations before you drop into the standard landing position described on page 195 (E, F, G).

The Delayed Axel

B

A

G

F

The Double Axel

For this jump, first performed in competition by Dick Button, you simply add another revolution to your turns in the air. Unless you have quite good height, you will have to make a few compromises.

More than likely, on the take-off you will not have time to allow your free leg to pass from behind all the way forward to its position parallel to the ice—unless, of course, you jump very high. Your delay as you lift into the air must be brief. This means that you must retract your arms into the rotational position sooner than you did on the single Axel. Since the motion of both the free leg and the arms contributes to the height of the jump, be careful not to shorten their movement too much, which would seriously reduce the height of the jump.

Do not forget to exert more effort on the spring than you did for the single Axel.

When you retract your arms in the air, their rotational position will have to be tighter. Since your rotations in the air will consequently be faster, you must check harder as you land. Remember to start the check just before your right foot hits the ice. If you have been practicing the delayed Axel with the maximum delay and, therefore, with a strong check, this will not be new to you.

The Triple Axel

As this is a double Axel with yet another revolution in the air, you simply do more of the same things that you did for the double Axel, with particular emphasis on rotation once you are airborne, and on a strong anticipatory check. As a practical matter, most skaters scrape the take-off edge on the triple Axel. This scrape occurs primarily because the rotation for the jump begins a split second earlier than it does for the double Axel, due to the need to complete three and a half revolutions in the air. Theoretically, jumping off a clean edge is possible—it simply requires a higher jump and faster rotation in the air. At the very least, this should be your goal.

The triple Axel was performed in competition for the first time in the 1978 World Championships by Vern Taylor of Canada.

Common Errors When Performing the Axel

Since the technique on the Axel must be precise (the jump being very sensitive to error), there are a large number of possible errors.

Landing on your right back inside edge is caused by:

- leaning out of the circle on the landing;
- bending your torso out of the circle on the landing;
- not checking the rotation sufficiently hard on the landing;
- dropping your free hip on the landing.

Leaning outside the circle in the air is caused by:

- your body or torso being outside the circle on the preparation edge, the transition, or the take-off;
- overrotating the shoulders as you take off;
- retracting your arms with the left elbow and shoulder down.

Skidding on the take-off edge is caused by:

- overrotating your shoulders or hips on the take-off;
- moving your arms too fast or too soon during the take-off.

Slipping off the take-off edge, in its worst form, will cause you to lose all control and to execute what is commonly known as a "waxel." When the toe pick of your skating foot does not dig into the ice as you lift off the ice, you will take off from the heel of the skating foot. The upward force of your arms and your free leg will throw the upper part of your body backward and outside the circle so forcefully that a fall is almost inevitable. The skating foot will be forced into the circle and out from under you. Any skater who has experienced this will know the sensation all too well and will do anything to prevent it from happening again! In this case, the pole vaulting action of the lift-off is absent. It is caused by:

- being outside the circle on the preparation or take-off edge;
- insufficient forward lean on the take-off edge;
- overrotating your shoulders and hips on the take-off;
- lifting your left arm too high on the actual lift-off.

Overrotating your shoulders on the take-off is caused by:

- your right arm swinging around during the take-off (young skaters frequently resort to this method in order to make sure sure that they get all the way around; don't worry; completed rotations happen automatically with sound technique);
- your free leg swinging around on the take-off;

- your head being too far over the left shoulder on the take-off edge;
- your left shoulder being too far back as you step onto the take-off edge;
- your left shoulder being too far forward on the preparation edge (this means that you will have to rotate the shoulders too much as you make the transition from the preparatory to the take-off edge).

Bending your free leg on the take-off edge is caused by:

- overrotating your shoulders on the take-off;
- leaning outside the circle on the take-off edge (in this case, a bent free leg can actually save you from doing a "waxel");
- insufficient concentration on keeping your free knee straight on the take-off.

Swinging the free leg around on the take-off is nearly impossible to stop, or even to slow down, once this motion is started, because of the relative weight of the leg. This is caused by:

- the right leg slipping behind the left leg during the transition (if this happens, your right leg will have to move in a circular path just to get around the skating leg; if the ice is relatively clean, you can often see the error in the markings on the ice);

The most common error when performing the Axel.
The dotted line shows the imprint on the ice created by the most common error associated with the Axel—stepping outside the circle created during the preparatory edge. This destroys the contiguous pattern of the preparation and take-off, and results both in the loss of some of the force for the jump and in the creation of forces that do not contribute to the jump's height and breadth.

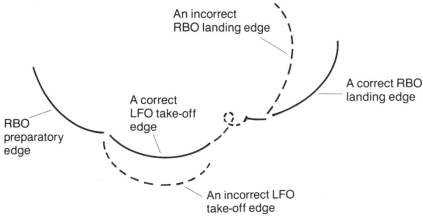

An incorrect
RBO landing edge

A correct RBO
landing edge

A correct
LFO take-off
edge

RBO
preparatory
edge

An incorrect LFO
take-off edge

- overrotating the shoulders at the beginning of the take-off edge, forcing the hips around, which in turn pulls the free leg around.

Insufficient forward lean on the take-off is caused by:

- insufficient backward extension of your free leg at the beginning of the take-off edge;
- lifting your arms too high as you step onto the take-off edge.

Insufficient rotation is caused by:

- insufficient height and breadth on the jump;
- insufficiently tight retraction of your arms and legs once in the air.

Insufficient delay on the delayed Axel is caused by:

- your head check being too brief;
- overrotating your shoulders or hips on the take-off;
- your right arm swinging around on the take-off;
- your free leg swinging around on the take-off.

Any of the foregoing can cause the jump to be lower than anticipated.

VARIATIONS ON THE AXEL

When you can do an ordinary or a delayed Axel consistently, try some of the variations. The technique on the preparation, the take-off, and the landing is the same for all Axels. All differences pertain to your position in the air.

The Tuck Axel

As you pull your arms into the rotational position, pull your legs up into a squat position.

The Cross Tuck

This is basically the same as a tuck Axel, except that you cross your legs as you bend them into the squat position.

The Open Axel

In this Axel, you remain more or less in the take-off position. Once in the air, retract your arms only slightly, as though you were holding a large beach ball. Since the arms are in a somewhat open position in the air, the check when you land is more difficult and requires greater strength and control than for an ordinary Axel. Spectators love this jump. The higher the jump, the greater the thrill for them.

G F E

The Reverse Delayed Axel

In this jump, the delay is at the end of the jump instead of at the beginning. Do an ordinary single Axel. After about three quarters of a turn, check your arms to slow down the last three quarters of the one and a half revolutions. Also, allow your legs to spread slightly. This technique will give the last part of your jump a feeling of suspension and will help you to execute a very smooth and fluid landing.

The Reverse Delayed Axel

D   C   B   A

The reverse delayed Axel begins with the spring preparation (A), the initiation of the spring (B), and the lift-off (C). Note the rapid retraction of the arms and right leg into the rotating position (D). At the peak of the jump, open up the arms and legs (E) and reach for the ice with the right foot (F). Your position should be open, not closed, on touchdown (G).

The Russian Split Axel

To do this jump, you must be able to do a delayed Axel. Take off as though you are doing a delayed Axel. Once in the air, reach for your toes just as you would for an ordinary Russian split (see page 267). After touching your toes, retract your arms and let your legs fall into the rotational position. To successfully execute this jump, your technique and timing must be infallible. I am aware of only one skater who was able to do this jump successfully and beautifully, Robin Cousins, the 1980 Olympic Gold Medalist.

THE SALCHOW

The Salchow consists of a take-off from a left back inside edge, one revolution in the air, and a landing on a right back outside edge. In the simplest terms, it is a waltz jump from a back inside edge. Ulrich Salchow of Sweden, who was World Champion 10 times between 1900 and 1911, invented this jump.

The Salchow has another story attached to it, which developed some years later. At the first post–World War II World Championships in Stockholm, Sweden, Dick Button won the Silver Medal even though he won the free-skating segment of the competition. Ulrich Salchow, impressed with Dick's performance and with his contribution to the sport of figure skating, told Dick that he should not leave the championship without a trophy. Ulrich invited Dick to his home to pick a trophy of his choosing. Dick, not wishing to offend Ulrich by taking the smallest and not wishing to appear too greedy by picking the largest, which was an equestrian statue featuring Peter the Great, chose a moderate-size trophy. In the spirit in which he received it, Dick determined to pass the trophy on to a young skater who he felt deserved to win a particular competition and who had made a significant contribution to the sport. Following the 1972 Olympic Games and World Championships, I received the trophy from Dick Button. I too shall someday pass it on to a deserving skater. I agree with Dick Button that such a skater must be "great," that is, someone who has changed the sport by being a part of it.

Although the Salchow is not difficult in most respects, the two challenges on this jump are timing and balance, because of the nature of the take-off edge. Since it is a left back inside edge, the weight of the free leg, being on the inside of the circle, tends to pull the body to the inside of the circle. If this is allowed to occur, you will be leaning too severely into the circle, and your jump will be low at best. In addition, the free leg is one of the important elements in lifting the body into the air. In order to accomplish its task, it must pass from inside the circle to the outside. Doing this without disturbing your balance is not easy. Consequently, the technique leading into the jump centers around maintaining balance and achieving the optimal timing for maximum lift.

You can achieve the proper setup for the Salchow through several different preparations:

- Stroke counterclockwise around the rink into a counterclockwise inside Mohawk for a right back outside preparatory edge.
- Do back crossovers counterclockwise, into a right back outside preparatory edge.
- Do back crossovers clockwise, into a right back inside preparatory edge.

In addition to these basic approaches, you can invent many other variations that will place you on a left back inside edge, in the proper position for the take-off. At the outset, I suggest that you follow the most basic approach, which is to stroke forward into an inside Mohawk.

The Preparation:

The one common element in all the preparations is the gradual rotation of the arms and shoulders on the preparatory edge. For example, after the inside Mohawk, your left arm is slightly in front and your right arm is slightly back. Your head should be facing away from the direction in which you are skating. You are on a bent right leg and skating on a back outside edge with your left leg extended comfortably behind you. Once in this position, allow your arms, shoulders, and head to rotate slowly counterclockwise. When your left arm is back and your right arm is in front, step onto the take-off leg. The important feature here is the gradual rotation in preparation for the step into the jump. This is in sharp contrast to the preparation for the Axel, in which it is important to halt the rotation on the preparatory edge.

On the step onto the left forward outside edge, move your left arm in front and your right arm out to the side. Extend your right leg comfortably behind. Once your weight is shifted completely to the left foot, allow your arms and shoulders to rotate counterclockwise at the same speed at which they rotated on the right back outside edge. This will create the rotational momentum necessary to perform the left forward outside three-turn into the take-off edge. Throughout this edge, the free leg should remain firmly behind and relatively straight. It should not be turned out.

When the rotation has progressed to a point where the three-turn can be done comfortably, execute it. Straighten the left leg slightly for the three-turn

218 and bend it again on exiting the turn. Your arm and shoulder check on the three-turn should be gentle, but not weak. You are now on a left back inside edge with your right arm back, left arm in front, and free leg back, slightly across and behind you. At this point, the most important issue is to keep your right hip up so that you are balanced directly over your left leg. To make this easier, turn your right leg in and bend it slightly. Keeping the right leg straight at this point can have disastrous consequences on the take-off, even though this is commonly attempted by skaters.

Immediately after the check, it is time to prepare for the lift-off.

The Take-Off:
Allow your arms, shoulders and head to rotate counterclockwise. The head should lead the rotation by looking over the left shoulder on the check of the three-turn. The rotation of the arms and shoulders should commence by more

The Salchow

A   B   C

H   I

or less bouncing off the check position and will follow the lead of the head. The free leg should come around from behind but should lag behind the rotation in the upper body. Keeping your free leg turned in and bent will help maintain the proper balance. About halfway through the rotation, begin to bend your left knee. Prior to this point, the left inside edge imprint on the ice should be virtually straight. The increased bend in the left knee, coupled with the rotation, will force the line of the edge to curve. Your shoulders should be at a 45-degree angle to your skating foot when you begin to increase the bend in your left knee. You should now begin to spring into the air.

Bring your arms back, then forward, in the elliptical path described for the waltz jump (see page 202). Pass your free leg in front of you, reaching out in much the same way as you did for the waltz jump. Spring from the left leg.

The take-off is surprisingly similar to that for the waltz jump. In fact, at the end of the back inside edge, you will do a three-turn and actually lift off

D

E

F

G

To perform a Salchow, stroke forward counterclockwise around the rink into an inside Mohawk for a right back outside preparatory edge. (You can also do back crossovers clockwise or counterclockwise into a right back preparatory edge.) Now step onto the take-off (left) leg, keeping your shoulders parallel to your hips (A). Rotate counterclockwise (B) into a left forward outside three-turn. Check the three-turn by moving the right arm and shoulder back. Keep the free (right) leg close to the ice (C). On the take-off, the left shoulder should be back (D). By the time you lift off, you will have completed a half turn (E). The rotation and landing are conventional (F, G, H, I).

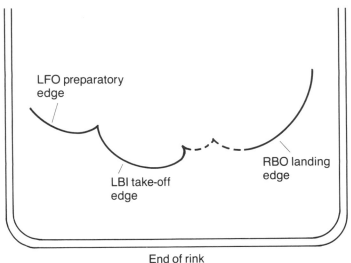

LFO preparatory edge

LBI take-off edge

RBO landing edge

End of rink

Pattern followed for a Salchow.

from the toe pick. Should you examine the imprint made by the take-off edge, you will find that there is a toe-pick mark on the ice at the end of the curved edge. This is expected and means that you have taken off going forward. Although this is not acknowledged officially, it also means that the actual rotation in the air is only half a revolution.

Since the single Salchow is similar to the waltz jump, you can keep your legs apart in the air. This will not impair your ability to land safely on a right back outside edge.

When you are first learning the Salchow, do it on relatively clean ice so you can examine the imprint on the take-off and the relationship between the take-off and landing edges. The left forward outside edge before the three-turn leading into the take-off edge should consist of only a gentle curve. Following the three-turn, the first two to four feet of the left back inside edge should be virtually straight. The length of the straight portion of the edge will be determined by your speed across the ice and the rate of the upper body and free leg motion on this edge. The absence of a straight line indicates either that you didn't check the three-turn properly or that you didn't stand directly over your skating leg, but were leaning into the circle. Where you began to bend and lift off, the edge will curve deeply. A straight line drawn tangent to the last two inches of the take-off edge should form a 90-degree angle with a line drawn tangent to the straight segment of the left back inside edge. Going beyond this on the take-off means either that you overrotated the upper body on the lift-off or that you lifted off too late. The landing edge should be on a line perpendicular to the end of the take-off edge. If you have gone beyond this line, you have not jumped out, but rather have jumped around. The upper body rotation on the take-off was therefore excessive and has, more than likely, resulted in a low jump.

The Double Salchow

To execute a double Salchow, simply contract into the rotational position once you are in the air. This means crossing the legs close together, bringing the arms in, and looking over the left shoulder.

The Delayed Double Salchow

The delayed double Salchow is merely the combination of a single Salchow take-off with a double Salchow rotational position. The most important aspect of the delayed double Salchow is the action of the right leg on the take-off. As you lift off the ice, reach out with the right leg. Also, hold your arms out as you would on a delayed Axel. After a split-second delay, contract quickly into the rotational position. Check hard on the landing.

The Triple and Quadruple Salchow

The only differences between the triple and quadruple Salchow and the double Salchow are 1) the time lapse between the take-off and the contraction into the rotational position and 2) the degree of contraction. Both must be quickened and accentuated: there must be less time to the contraction and a much tighter rotational position in the air.

Common Errors When Performing the Salchow

Many of the errors made in the execution of the Salchow involve timing and balance. These mistakes generally result in a jump that is not very high, or in which the body is off balance in the air, making it difficult to land properly. Timing is essential for a proper lift-off and for balance. The upward motion of the arms and free leg, and the timing of the rotation of the upper body on the take-off edge, are aimed at placing the body over the skating leg and positioning the upper body to face the direction of flight. In the absence of proper timing and balance, you will not jump high, nor will you be balanced in the air. There are many specific problems to watch for.

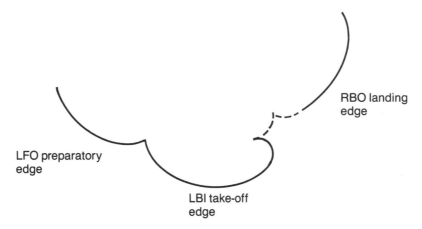

RBO landing
edge

LFO preparatory
edge

LBI take-off
edge

Unnecessary rotational motion for a Salchow.
An excessively long preparatory edge and/or a curved take-off edge deflects some of the power for the jump into unnecessary rotational motion throughout the jump.

An inability to control the rotation on the landing is caused by:

- an insufficiently strong arm and shoulder check on the landing;
- a too-open rotating position in the air;
- a free leg motion on the take-off that occurs too far away from the skating leg.

Leaning into the circle created by the right back outside landing edge, perhaps even falling to the right, is caused by:

- not allowing sufficient time on the take-off edge for the upper body to rotate to a position facing the direction of flight;
- dropping the right hip or shoulder on the take-off edge;
- lunging forward at the waist on the take-off;
- leaning into the circle on the take-off edge, which means that the first part of the left back inside edge was curved rather than straight.

A low jump is caused by:

- lack of spring on the take-off;
- the absence of a synchronized lifting motion by the arms and free leg, and the left leg spring;
- the upper body not facing in the direction of flight;

- leaning in or dropping your right hip or shoulder on the take-off;
- a free leg motion on the take-off that occurs too far away from the skating leg.

A take-off edge with too much toe-pick involvement, producing a deep rut in the ice on the curved part of the take-off edge, is caused by:

- a wide free leg swing on the take-off;
- dropping the right hip or shoulder on the take-off;
- leaning forward on the take-off;
- rotating the upper body insufficiently by the time lift-off occurs;
- swinging the arms around on the take-off rather than in a down-up elliptical path.

Not facing the upper body in the direction of the jump is caused by:

- not leading with the head following the three-turn into the take-off edge;
- taking off too early;
- rotating too slowly after the left forward outside three-turn.

Dropping the right hip or shoulder on the take-off edge is caused by:

- turning the free leg out as it passes around the skating leg during the take-off;
- skating a curved edge immediately after the left forward outside three-turn;
- lunging forward at the waist;
- rotating the upper body too rapidly on the take-off edge.

A take-off edge that does not have the toe-pick mark at the end is caused by:

- insufficient upper body rotation prior to lift-off;
- the free leg motion anticipating or lagging behind the actual lift-off;
- generally poor timing on the take-off.

Difficulty in the timing on the lift-off is caused by:

- ill-timed upper body rotation after the left forward outside three-turn;
- absence of the ricochet motion on the three-turn check, to initiate the rotation for lift-off;
- insufficient or excessive rotation into the left forward outside three-turn.

THE LOOP

The loop jump consists of a take-off from a right back outside edge, a single revolution in the air, and a landing on the same edge. Its origin is attributed to Werner Rittberger, who placed second in the World Championships from 1910 to 1912, and is known as a "Rittberger" in Europe. However, there is some evidence that it might have been first performed by others in the 1890s.

The loop jump is particularly useful as a way of learning the basic rotational position: legs crossed, arms retracted, and head over the left shoulder. This is largely a function of the preparation technique and of the take-off.

The main aspect of any preparation for a loop jump is the control of the rotation leading into the jump. Nearly all preparation for the loop involves counterclockwise rotation, be they three-turns or inside Mohawks. The key is to control the rotation of the upper body so that the body is in the proper position at the time of lift-off. Your primary goal will be to prevent the upper body from rotating ahead of the inherent rotation of the edge. If you do not control the rotation, it will cause you to pull the edge around and lose your balance.

While there are many preparations, one done on a large circle is particularly useful for the beginner. In rinks used for hockey, circles are drawn on the ice at the ends. These can be used as a guide for this preparation.

The Preparation:
The preparation consists of a pair of left forward outside three-turns. After the first three-turn, step onto a right back outside edge. Step forward onto a left forward outside edge and repeat the process. This fairly simple description represents only the bare bones of the preparation process. Several subtleties are critical to a successful jump.

First, as in the case of the Salchow, timing is of primary importance. For the loop, the timing relates primarily to the speed of the upper body rotations on the preparations, relative to the three-turn sequence, which should be synchronized.

Second, the rotation of the upper body throughout the preparation should be continuous. If you were able to observe yourself from above, you should see your arms rotating counterclockwise at a constant speed.

Third, due to the constant rotation, there are no checks on the three-turns during the preparation. Strictly speaking, the arms and shoulders remain out to the side and the upper body is square with the hips throughout the entire preparation. It can be helpful to imagine that you are holding a very large beach ball in front of you as you prepare.

Fourth, the head remains facing forward throughout the preparation.

Finally, the preparation is performed on bent knees, except for the rise over the left leg for the three-turns.

The Step:

After the second three-turn, the next step brings you onto the take-off edge (the right back outside edge). This step will establish the leg positions that will prevail throughout the jump. Therefore the step is of great importance.

Following the second three-turn, turn your right foot out and place it one to two feet to the side of the left foot. At the instant that you place your right foot on the ice, it should feel as if you are squatting with your legs apart. As your weight is shifted gradually to your right foot, it will glide at about a 30- to 45-degree angle behind and across the imprint of your left foot. Keeping the feet turned out means that they will be moving in slightly different directions. As your right foot glides behind, your left foot crosses over, turned out. Bend your right knee deeply. Your left leg will bend almost as much. You should be on the ball of the foot.

During the weight shift, your arms are out to the side. The squat in your knees should force you to lean forward, with your back arched and your chin up.

The Take-Off:

As you begin to spring off your right leg, your left foot will leave the ice and remain crossed in front. During the lift-off, continue rotating the upper body. By the time you leave the ice, therefore, your body will be facing in the direction of the jump. This will result in a toe-pick mark at the end of the take-off edge similar to the one made during the Salchow. This also means that the jump effectively consists of only half a revolution in the air. To help you lift into the air, lower your arms slightly as you bend into the spring position and raise them on the lift-off. As you lift off, contract your arms into the rotational position and turn your head over your left shoulder.

After about three quarters of a turn, prepare to land on a right back outside edge, as described on page 195.

When you are first learning the loop jump, it is useful to examine the take-off edge after completing the jump. Try to do the jump on relatively clean ice so that the imprint shows up clearly. You should observe the following:

1. The beginning of the take-off edge will have only a slight curve, will begin two to three feet to the right of the preparatory edge, and will run at about a 45-degree angle to it.

The Loop Jump

A   B   C

As you prepare for a loop jump, let your arms remain out to the side (A). As you begin to shift your weight to your right foot, keep your hips open, with your feet at a 45-degree angle to each other (B). Keep the feet apart as you prepare for the lift-off (C). Move your arms downward in a scooping motion for the take-off (D). On the take-off, your legs should already be crossed (E). Retract into a tight rotating position (F). Land, after the rotation, in the manner described on page 229.

Note: It is also possible to check your rotation before the take-off by moving the right shoulder firmly back (G).

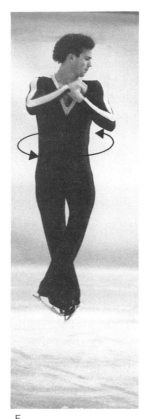

D   E   F   G

Pattern followed for a loop jump.

Direction
of movement ➡

LBI preparatory
edge

RBO take-off
edge

RBO landing
edge

2. As the take-off edge crosses over the preparatory edge, the curvature of the edge should deepen, that is, the circle created by the take-off edge should become smaller.

3. At the end of the take-off edge, you should observe a toe-pick mark which, if extrapolated, would indicate that a three-turn was about to occur had you not lifted off. The absence of a toe-pick mark indicates that you have not rotated sufficiently to face the jump on the lift-off.

4. The point of touchdown should be directly across from the toe-pick mark on a line drawn approximately from the crossover point of the preparatory and take-off edges, through the toe-pick mark on the take-off, to the touchdown point.

An examination of the print on the ice can highlight problems or mistakes. Deviations from the imprint described here can indicate specific errors in your technique.

The Open Loop

The open loop represents a more dramatic form of the basic loop jump. The principal difference is the position in the air, which consists of the arms remaining out to the side and the legs open and apart.

To accomplish this position in the air, you must make several adjustments to your technique on the actual lift-off. As you spring off your right leg, pass your left leg to the side, reaching out in the direction of the jump. Extend your left leg as you do this. Instead of retracting your arms, lift them out to the side in an open position as you lift off, leaving them out throughout the jump. About halfway through the jump, bring your feet together, left crossed over right, to complete the rotation and prepare for a conventional landing on a right back outside edge.

The Loop Sequence

Doing basic loop jumps one after another in sequences of two or more provides an excellent method for improving your timing on the jump and for preparing to learn the double loop. Since you land on the same edge that you use for the take-off, the landing of the first loop is the preparation for the spring into the second.

The take-off on subsequent loop jumps is quite straightforward but requires a catlike springing action into the air. In fact, if you have seen a deer leaping in flight across a field, you will have observed the action needed for a sequence of loop jumps. As you prepare to land the first loop, begin opening your arms a little earlier than normal—at the peak of the jump. When you touch down, your arms should be out to the side, and your head should be facing forward. Leave your left leg in front and crossed over the right. Bend your right knee to cushion the landing and simultaneously allow your arms to move downward in preparation for the lift-off into the jump. When you have reached the maximum bend, spring into the second loop, using the same technique that you employed for the first jump. Repeat the process for each subsequent loop jump.

The Double Loop

For the double loop, merely add another revolution in the air. Be careful not to try too hard. Exerting too much force on the take-off can disturb the timing and balance and prevent a successful execution. Any additional force should occur on the contraction into the rotational position once you are in the air.

The Triple and Quadruple Loop

Add an additional revolution to the double loop jump for the triple, and another to the triple for the quadruple. The principal difference is the tightness of the rotational position in the air. Dick Button was responsible for another first, executing the first successful triple loop in competition.

Other Methods for Executing the Loop

Some subtleties during the take-off have been adopted for the loop by skaters with substantial expertise. The most prevalent change applies to the technique for the step onto the take-off edge. Many skaters will stop the continuous rotation at this point by checking the last three-turn leading to the take-off edge. This check places the right arm back and the left arm in front. The left foot remains to the side on the ice until the skater secures his or her balance. The skater then bends the right knee for the lift-off, and the remaining technique is the same as for the standard loop jump.

This technique is certainly suitable for skaters of considerable expertise.

The principal difficulty is that the shoulders must rotate 180 degrees from the check position to the take-off position during the spring part of the take-off edge, a relatively short period of time. This rotation produces considerable force and can easily throw the body off balance, particularly since proper balance on the take-off edge requires very fine control of all the forces. Common mistakes are: dropping the right shoulder on the take-off, which occasionally leads to slipping off the edge and an unpleasant fall on the right hip; overrotation at the time of lift-off, forcing you to abort the jump; and an insufficiently tight position in the air. Because there is greater rotational force using this technique, the take-off movements are more difficult to control and to time correctly. Without substantial practice, consistency is more difficult to achieve. However, this method does permit a higher and longer jump than does the basic technique.

Common Errors When Performing a Loop

The errors referred to in this section apply primarily to the basic technique for a loop jump. As more revolutions are added, the more sensitive the jump becomes to the following technical mistakes.

Inward lean during the landing is caused by:

- dropping the right arm and shoulder on the take-off;
- not leaning forward sufficiently on the take-off edge until the actual lift-off;
- stopping the rotation on the preparation or on the step onto the take-off edge.

A low jump is caused by:

- poor timing of the arms, upper body rotation, and spring on the take-off;
- not leaning sufficiently far forward prior to the actual lift-off;
- leaning into the circle on the take-off edge;
- overrotating the upper body at the time of lift-off.

Overrotation on the take-off is caused by:

- fast upper body rotation on the preparation;
- too slow a lift-off;
- an around-and-in arm motion on the spring, instead of down, up, and in—the proper "scoop" motion.

Difficulty in crossing your legs in the air is caused by:

- not turning your left leg out after the step onto the take-off edge;
- not placing your right foot to the side and turned out as you step onto the take-off edge;
- not rotating the upper body far enough to face the jump on the take-off.

Leaning into the circle on the take-off edge is caused by:

- lowering your right arm and shoulder as you step onto the take-off edge;
- not turning your right leg out on the step onto the take-off edge;
- not leaning forward in a squatting position on the step onto the take-off edge;
- not turning your left leg out as you prepare for lift-off.

THE INSIDE AXEL

The inside Axel consists of a take-off from a right forward inside edge, one and a half revolutions in the air, and a landing on a right back outside edge. It was invented by Austrian Willi Boeckl, four times World Champion.

Pattern followed for an inside Axel.

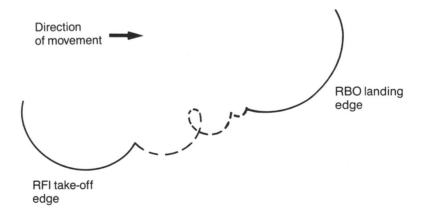

By itself, the inside Axel is not a particularly dramatic jump. This is because of the placement of the body on the take-off and the effect that that has on the take-off edge. A take-off from a forward inside edge means that the free leg is on the inside of the circle created by the edge. In this position, the free leg cannot pass forward to aid in the spring from the ice, since it would be moving in a direction opposite to the inherent rotation of the edge and the jump. Since the free leg must remain virtually passive, the rotational movement of the upper body and arms creates a very deep take-off edge. Therefore, most of the force is rotational, leaving little force available to lift into the air. For these reasons, the inside Axel is most frequently used as part of a more complex jump sequence.

The preparation edge for the inside Axel is a left forward inside edge. Move your left arm and shoulder in front, and your right arm and shoulder back. Face forward. Your right leg should be in front, but it will move to the side about two feet from your left foot just before the step onto the take-off edge.

As you step to the side on a right forward inside edge, right foot pointing straight ahead, deeply bend your right knee. Bring your arms to your sides. Leave your left leg to the side and slightly bent; it will feel as though it is dangling to the side.

As you spring, scoop your arms down, then up into the rotational position. Bring the left knee toward the right knee. The take-off edge will curve deeply. At the very end of the take-off edge, the toe pick strikes the ice. In fact, you may even do a fraction of a turn on the right toe pick as you lift into the air.

After one and a half revolutions in the air, land in the conventional manner on a right back outside edge.

While the inside Axel is not a particularly exhilarating jump, it can be very effective when incorporated in the context of other maneuvers. If you do this, remember that the fundamental inside Axel technique remains the same, even though the preparatory edge differs.

THE WALLEY

The Walley is an edge jump in which the direction of the rotation of the take-off edge is different from the direction of rotation in the air. It consists of a take-off from a right back inside edge, one counterclockwise revolution in the air, and a landing on the right back outside edge.

Some dispute surrounds the identification of the inventor. The British believe it was invented by a Scot named Pat Low, while Americans believe fellow countryman Nate Walley was responsible for its creation. Regardless of the inventor, figure skating is better off with the Walley jump.

While it is difficult to attain substantial height on this jump, a sequence of Walleys down the ice at great speed can be an effective part of an overall program. Furthermore, they can be useful as part of a jump combination.

The most effective way to approach the take-off edge of a Walley is through a counterclockwise inside Mohawk: a right forward inside edge followed by a left back inside edge. There should be little rotation and no check on the Mohawk itself. Remain on the left back inside edge for only a second.

The action begins as you step onto the right back inside edge. This step should be to the side and relatively wide, about two feet from the left foot. As you step, swing your right arm and shoulder back and your left arm across in front of your body. Place the left leg, which is bent, behind you. Bend the right knee deeply.

To lift off, spring from the right leg. As you lift, pull back and to the side with the knee of the left leg. Simultaneously, swing your left arm back and your right arm down and up in the path that crosses in front of your body. Look to the left.

Once you are in the air, contract your arms into a rotating position. Since your left leg has led the body into the air, and since you are rotating only one revolution, it is unlikely that you will be able to cross your legs in the typical rotating position. Rather, they will remain side by side and close together in the air.

The landing is a conventional right back outside edge, but with one exception. Since the legs did not cross, the left leg will pass from the side into the normal landing position.

Walleys can be executed sequentially in much the same way that loops can. The difference is that the landing of the first Walley is separate from the take-off of the second. After landing on the right back outside edge, change your arm positions to the windup position for the take-off by rotating the arms clockwise. Simultaneously change to a right back inside edge. Crossing your left leg across the print behind you and dropping your left shoulder ever so slightly will help you effect the edge change. Proceed with the next Walley.

The Walley

A

B

Enter a Walley from a Mohawk (A). Look over your right shoulder as you perform the Mohawk (B). As you step on the right back inside edge, rotate your arms and shoulders clockwise (C). Lift your left leg to the side, and rotate your arms and shoulders counterclockwise on the take-off (D). Once in the air, contract your arms into a rotating position, and let your legs remain side by side and close together as you rotate.

C

D

Pattern followed for a Walley.

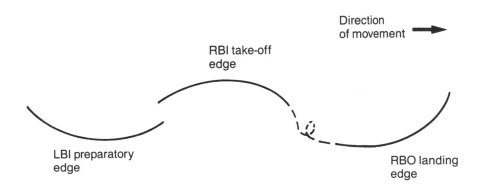

RBI take-off
edge

Direction
of movement →

LBI preparatory
edge

RBO landing
edge

15

Toe Jumps

All toe jumps—with one exception, the Lutz—are edge jumps with a toe assist by the other foot on take-off. They are similar to their respective edge jumps in terms of the take-off edge. However, because both feet are on the ice at the time of take-off, the technique is markedly different.

One important difference is that the leg with the toe pick in the ice at the time of the take-off acts as a pole vault. (On edge jumps, it was only the toe pick of the take-off foot that acted as a pole vault.) This has two important implications: 1) the pole-vaulting action on toe jumps is more powerful and central to the jump, and 2) the half revolution advantage inherent in the take-off for edge jumps does not occur at the time of lift-off on toe jumps. Nearly all toe jumps consist of revolutions that are theoretically and practically multiples of one—no half revolutions.

THE TOE LOOP

As the name suggests, the toe loop is a loop jump with a toe-assisted take-off. It consists of a right back outside edge, a left toe assist, one revolution in the air, and a right back outside edge landing. The simple toe loop is the easiest of the toe jumps, for one reason: The upper body and hips rotate half a revolution on the take-off, making it easier to complete the required one revolution in the air. This is one of the reasons why the first clean quadruple executed in competition was the quadruple toe loop. (It was successfully performed by Kurt Browning of Canada at the 1988 World Championships.)

Toe-assisted jumps allow a skater to attain great height and rotational power.

The Toe Loop

A

B

C

H

I

On the left forward inside edge in preparation for the toe loop, position your right arm and shoulder back and your left arm and shoulder forward (A). Step on a right forward inside edge and rotate counterclockwise into a three-turn (B). Following the three-turn, keep the shoulders virtually square (perpendicular to the skating foot), and reach back with the left leg (C). On the take-off, the shoulders rotate counterclockwise to a position parallel to the skating foot (D). Scoop your arms in toward your chest as you take off, execute one revolution (E), and land in the conventional manner (F, G, H, I).

D E F G

Pattern followed for a toe loop.

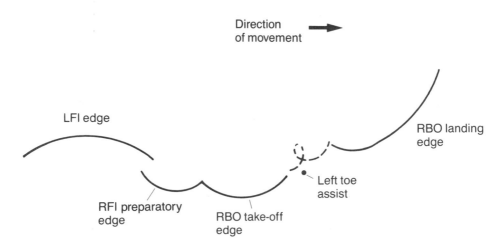

The Preparation:

The preparation for a toe loop consists of a left forward inside edge. On the preparation edge, the left arm and shoulder are in front and the right arm and shoulder back. Extend the free foot about two feet in front of the left foot.

In preparation for the step onto the take-off foot, gradually begin to rotate your arms and shoulders counterclockwise. By the time you are ready to step onto the right foot, your upper body should be square, with your arms out to the side.

The Step:

The step onto the take-off foot is an important part of the preparation. Reach to the side with your right foot, placing it on the ice about two feet from the left foot. Place the right foot on a right forward inside edge. As you shift your weight, lift your left foot behind you. The positioning of the left foot behind is critical, since lifting it from the side would mean that it must travel a great distance to be in the appropriate position for the take-off. This in turn creates unwanted rotational momentum on the take-off edge.

The Windup:

After the step, begin gently to rotate your arms and shoulders counterclockwise. Allow your left leg to move behind the skating leg. The left leg motion will provide the primary rotational momentum required to execute a right forward inside three-turn. The right forward inside edge should be fairly short, about three to five feet depending on your speed across the ice. It should also have only a gentle curve to it.

After the right forward inside three-turn, extend your free leg back and slightly to the side. This will be possible only if you have not allowed the free leg to swing around on the three-turn. Check the shoulders by rotating them clockwise. Your left arm and shoulder should now be in front of you, your right arm to the side and slightly back. Bend your right knee deeply.

The Take-Off:

The actual lift entails a number of simultaneous actions. Begin by bringing your arms down, rotating them counterclockwise. Place the left toe pick in the ice directly behind you with your left leg straight. Your left toe should not be placed across and behind the right foot—in other words, across the imprint on the ice. Spring from the right leg and scoop the arms up and into the rotational position. Execute one revolution in the air and land in the conventional manner.

Once again, examining the imprint on the ice is helpful in determining whether or not you have employed the correct take-off technique. The left preparatory edge should have only a gentle curve to it, as should the right forward inside edge before the three-turn. Watch for a right forward inside edge that lasts too long. If it does, chances are that you will have too much upper body rotation prior to the three-turn.

Following the three-turn, the right back outside take-off edge should have slightly more curve. The toe-pick mark should be outside the circle created by the right back outside edge. A toe-pick mark on the inside of the circle means either that the left leg has swung around, ending up too far behind the right leg, or that the arm and shoulder check was insufficient following the three-turn. The landing edge should be approximately on a line connecting the tip of the three-turn, the end of the take-off edge, and the point of touchdown.

The Double Toe Loop

The double toe loop is merely a single toe loop with an additional revolution. In the air, the contraction into the rotational position must be somewhat more severe.

The Triple Toe Loop

This is a double loop with one more revolution. The rotational position must be substantially higher.

The Quadruple Toe Loop

The take-off on the quadruple toe loop must be fairly energetic. In addition, the contraction into the rotational position occurs immediately after the lift-off. In the air, the body position must be tight, particularly the legs, which must be very close together. Nevertheless, it is not impossible to move from the triple to the quadruple toe loop.

4 revolutions

3 revolutions

2 revolutions

F   E   D

Brian Boitano performing a quadruple toe loop. Note the energy and tight rotational position required for the jump.

1¼ revolutions

C

B

A

H

G

**Common Errors When Performing
the Toe Loop**

Since the control of rotational momentum on the right back outside take-off edge is the critical feature of the toe loop, the most frequent errors relate to the speed of rotation on the preparation and its timing relative to lift-off. In this sense the errors are very similar to those confronted on a loop jump. The inability to control rotation can make it difficult to achieve height and can create forces that result in a fall or in loss of control on the landing.

Landing on a right back inside edge is caused by:

- not checking the rotation early enough in the air, causing you to overrotate the jump;
- swinging the right arm across the body on the take-off, a motion that can pull the upper body outside the circle on the take-off;
- rotating the upper body too far on the take-off.

Leaning too far to the right on the landing, or even slipping off the landing edge, is caused by:

- dropping the right shoulder on the take-off;
- passing the arm downward too severely on the take-off;
- bending forward at the waist as you reach back to place the left toe in the ice;
- leaning in too far on the right back outside edge.

A low toe jump is caused by:

- not rotating the upper body a full quarter turn by the time of lift-off;
- bending the left leg as the toe pick is placed in the ice;
- placing your left toe too close to the right foot, or across behind it;
- hammering the toe into the ice instead of placing it on the ice in the manner of a pole vault;
- placing the toe in the ice either before or after the initiation of the spring action from the right leg;
- poor timing of the spring relative to the placement of the toe pick in the ice and relative to the scooping motion of the arms on lift-off.

Left toe-pick placement behind the right leg and across the take-off edge is caused by:

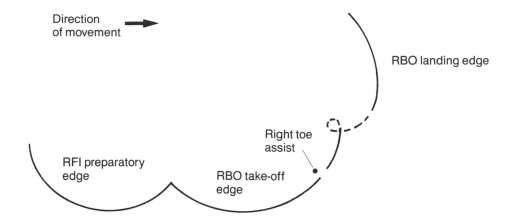

Swinging the free leg too wide while performing the three-turn for a toe loop.
When the free leg swings too wide on the three-turn for a toe loop, the pattern shown here results. This error produces an excessive amount of rotational force as you enter the take-off.

- swinging the free leg as you perform the three-turn;
- a strong arm and shoulder check on the three-turn, which forces the left leg back as a counterforce;
- picking the left leg up to the side on the step from the preparatory edge onto the right forward inside edge;
- spending too much time on the right forward inside edge before the three-turn.

A skid on the right back outside edge is caused by:

- rotating the upper body too far around prior to lift-off;
- swinging both the free leg and the free hip around on the three-turn.

THE TOE WALLEY

Unlike the Walley edge jump, the toe Walley is quite common. It consists of a left-toe-assisted right back inside edge take-off, one counterclockwise revolution in the air, and a landing on the right back outside edge. The toe Walley is often considered easier than the toe loop, but this is probably an illusion. Many skaters do not actually perform a toe Walley but rather a toe loop. Because the inherent rotation of the take-off edge is opposite to the rotation of the jump (a counter-like motion), it is reasonably difficult to remain on the right

A   B   C   D

I

The Toe Walley

The preparation for a toe Walley requires strong, well-defined shoulder positions. The left arm and shoulder are forward, the right arm and shoulder back and to the side (A). After a left forward outside three-turn, reach to the side with your right foot (B). Rotate your arms and shoulders clockwise for the lift-off (C). Begin the lift-off with a downward and counterclockwise motion of the arms. When the shoulders are perpendicular to the skating foot, place your left toe pick on the ice and begin to spring from the right leg. As you lift off, your head should be turned over your left shoulder and your arms should begin their scooping motion (D). Once in the air, contract your arms and legs into the rotational position (E, F). After one revolution, land on the right back outside edge (G, H, I).

E   F   G   H

back inside edge until the point of lift-off. Many skaters inadvertently change to a back outside edge near the end of the take-off. The reasons for this will become clear as the description of the technique unfolds.

The Preparation:

The preparation for the toe Walley is different from that employed for the toe loop. Skate down the length of the ice. Step onto a left forward outside edge, with your left arm and shoulder more or less in front and your right arm and shoulder to the side. Rotate the arms and shoulders counterclockwise. The right leg should be back but not straight. The line of this edge should have only a gentle curve to it.

When your arms and shoulders have rotated to the point that your left arm and shoulder are back and your right arm and shoulder are in front, execute a left forward outside three-turn. As you exit the three-turn, gently check the turn, rotating your right arm and shoulder to the side and your left arm and shoulder slightly in front. After the check, keep your right foot near the left leg in preparation for the step onto the take-off edge. You should now be on a left back inside edge.

The Step:

To make the step onto the take-off edge, reach to the side with your right foot. As you do, rotate your arms and shoulders clockwise, so that your right arm and shoulder are back and your left arm and shoulder are in front. You should make this movement relatively forcefully. Drop your left shoulder ever so slightly, and as you step onto the right back inside edge, bend the right knee deeply.

Once you have shifted your weight completely to your right foot, extend your left leg back and slightly to the side in preparation for the placement of the left toe pick into the ice. This motion should take relatively little time.

The Take-Off:

The lift-off itself begins with the downward and counterclockwise motion of the arms. When the shoulders are perpendicular to the skating foot, place your left toe pick in the ice and begin to spring from the right leg. Continue your arms' counterclockwise rotation; your arms should now begin a scooping-like motion. As you lift off, move your head over your left shoulder. By the time you take off, your upper body and hips should have rotated a full quarter turn.

Once in the air, contract into the conventional rotational position. After rotating one revolution, land on a right back outside edge.

The pattern of the preparation, take-off, and landing of this jump approximates a straight line. However, the line of all the edges boasts a gentle curve. The most important edge is, of course, the right back inside edge take-off. As mentioned at the outset, it is very difficult to maintain a true right back inside edge up to the time of lift-off. The reason: the direction of rotation on the jump is opposite to the direction of rotation of the take-off edge. The rotation inherent in the take-off edge is clockwise, whereas the direction of rotation in the jump is counterclockwise. Since the rotational force for the jump increases as you approach lift-off, it becomes increasingly difficult to hold the back inside edge— the right foot wants to follow the path of least resistance, which is to change to a back outside edge. While such a change of edge is technically incorrect, it occurs, and is generally not noticed in competitive events, primarily because it is so difficult to discern. However, the skater striving for perfection should be aware of this problem.

The Double Toe Walley

This is a single toe Walley with one more revolution added in the air.

The Triple and Quadruple Toe Walley

Add one more revolution in the air to the double toe Walley and you will have a triple. Add another for the quadruple. Naturally, more energy, strength, and precision are required to successfully accomplish the triple and quadruple toe Walleys.

Common Errors When Performing the Toe Walley

Errors frequently confronted in the toe Walley are similar to those for the toe loop. The main difference is that the left leg is easier to control, since it does not swing around on the three-turn leading into the take-off edge. The principal problem relates to body position: balancing the opposing rotational forces while trying to remain on a right back inside edge is a difficult and delicate task. Exaggerating any of these positions can throw the jump off balance.

The common problems on the toe Walley have causes that are virtually identical to the causes of problems on the toe loop, and don't need to be described again (see page 244). However, watch for these particular errors:

- dropping the left shoulder too much during the right back inside take-off edge;
- swinging the arms around on the take-off, instead of scooping them;
- looking over the left shoulder too early on the take-off;
- lifting the free leg too high behind you, causing you to lunge forward as you extend it in preparation for the pole-vaulting action;
- leaning too far forward as you bend for the spring, causing you to drop your right shoulder as you rotate your arms and scoop them toward your body for the lift-off.

THE FLIP

The flip jump is simply a toe-assisted Salchow. It consists of a take-off from a left back inside edge with a right toe assist, one counterclockwise revolution in the air, and a landing on a right back outside edge. The origin of the jump is attributed to Bruce Mapes, an amateur skater in the 1920s who became a professional skater with the Ice Follies in the 1930s. Although the flip was known for many years as a Mapes, it is not indisputable that Bruce Mapes was the inventor. In Europe, it is called a toe Salchow.

The addition of a toe assist to the basic Salchow dramatically changes the technique on the jump. Unlike the Salchow, the pattern for the flip is based on a relatively straight line, and therefore it is best performed on a line going the length of the rink. In addition, it requires a complete revolution in the air.

A   B   C

G   H   I   J   K

The Flip Jump

In this sequence, Brian Boitano performs a triple flip jump. The right arm and shoulder are back, and the left arm and shoulder are forward on a flip jump (A). As you change the edge on the preparation, rotate the arms and shoulders counterclockwise (B). Hold the left forward outside edge for only a short distance as you rotate for the three-turn (C). Check the three-turn with a firm backward twist of the right arm and shoulder (D). As you extend the right leg behind you after the three-turn, deeply bend your left knee; this forces your upper body forward. To initiate the take-off, plant your right toe pick on the ice (E). As you start to rise up and off the ice, move your right arm forward and your left arm back (F). As your arms pass by your body, turn your head to the left (G). Once in the air, move your arms into the rotational position and cross your left leg over your right (H). Rotate your body and land on a right back outside edge (I, J, K, L, M).

D

E

F

L

M

Pattern followed for a flip jump.

RBO landing
edge

Right toe assist

LFI preparatory
edge

Right toe
push-off

LFO preparatory
edge

LBI take-off
edge

Direction
of movement

The Preparation:

The preparation edge is executed on the foot from which you will take off. Skate a left forward inside edge with a gentle curve. On this edge, place your left arm and shoulder in front of you and your right arm and shoulder back. Your right leg should be straight in front of your left leg, toe pointed, with the foot several inches above the ice. You need to bend the left leg only slightly. Your hips should form a line perpendicular to the skating foot. Look in the direction in which you are skating.

To change to the second part of the preparation edge, bring your right foot alongside the left and push with the right toe pick. As you do this, change your arm and shoulder position so that after the push, your right arm and shoulder are in front and your left arm and shoulder are back. When changing your arm position, the arms should pass close to the body, almost in a walking motion. Change the edge as you push, so you are now skating on a left forward outside edge with your right leg behind you. Bend your left knee more than you did on the inside edge. This edge also should have only a gentle curve to it.

The Windup:

This motion should create sufficient rotational momentum to permit the easy execution of a left forward outside three-turn, which will place you on the left back inside take-off edge. As you enter the three-turn, straighten your left leg to ease yourself over the turn.

The clockwise arm and shoulder check on the three-turn will result in your right arm and shoulder being back and the left arm and shoulder being in front of you. This position should be quite firm, even severe, resulting in the shoulders creating a line parallel to the skating foot. To accomplish the change in the arm positions, the arms should pass relatively close to the body.

Following the three-turn, your right leg should be extended straight behind you in preparation for its pole-vaulting function. As you extend the right leg, bend the left knee deeply. As you bend the left knee, your upper body will be forced forward. Simply make certain that your back is arched and your chin is up. You should now be looking straight ahead, opposite the direction in which you are skating.

The Take-Off:

A successful take-off depends on perfect timing of the arm motion, the placement of the toe on the ice, the rotation of the shoulders, and the lift-off. All of these actions must be timed in a way that allows them to reach an end point simultaneously. While the initiation of each movement may differ in time by a split second, it will feel as if they begin at the same time. Place the right toe pick on the ice. Change the arm positions yet again, by passing them close to the body in a walking fashion, moving the right arm and shoulder in front and the left arm and shoulder back. Your hands will end up in a position no higher than the top of your head as you leave the ice. As your arms pass by your body, begin to move your head over the left shoulder. The action of the arms passing by the body plus the turning of the head rotates the shoulders and creates the rotational momentum necessary to accomplish the revolution in the air.

Once in the air, retract your arms into the rotational position and cross your left leg inside your right. Prepare and land on a conventional right back outside edge.

The Double Flip

The double flip is merely a single flip with an additional revolution in the air. When you are learning the double flip, try not to be overly concerned about rotation, because this can lead to one of the most common errors in the double flip: the arms passing around the body instead of close to it and in a premature retraction into the rotational position. This causes the upper body to rotate too far on take-off and prevents the skater from realizing the potential of the springing motion.

To counteract this problem, try to execute a brief delay in rotation after lift-off. The walking-like motion of the arms is designed to enable you to do this. When your arms reach the end point (the right extended forward, the left back, with the hands no higher than the head), hold them in that position for a split second. Then retract them into the rotational position.

The Triple Flip

The triple flip is a double flip with one more revolution in the air. By the time you have the skill to approach the triple, you should have achieved a level of technical expertise that will preclude any concern about overrotation on the take-off. This will enable you to retract your arms into a rotational position immediately after lift-off.

F

E

D

J

C

B

A

I

H

G

Following the conventional preparation for a delayed double flip (A, B, C), bend your left leg to its maximum (D). Even after the take-off, keep your arms out (E). After a complete rotation with your arms out (F), retract them into the rotating position (G). Note the crossed position of the left leg over the right during the rotation (H). The landing remains conventional (I, J).

Common Errors When Performing the Flip

Leaning too far to the right (that is, to the inside of the circle) on the landing is caused by:

- contracting into the rotational position with the right arm and elbow lower than the left arm and elbow;
- tilting the head to the right as you take off;
- dropping the right shoulder on the take-off.

Dropping your right shoulder on the take-off is caused by:

- not raising your right arm high enough during the upward motion of the arms;
- placing greater force on the downward motion of the right arm than on the downward motion of the left at the beginning of the lift-off motion;
- passing the arms around the body with the right elbow too low during the take-off;
- leaning in too far on the take-off edge, creating an edge with too much curve;
- lunging too far forward with the upper body on the take-off.

Difficulty in achieving height on the jump is caused by:

- poorly timed arm motion, shoulder rotation, toe assist, and spring from the left leg;
- passing the arms around rather than close to the body, so that they cannot contribute to the upward motion on the lift-off;
- bending the right leg as the right toe pick contacts the ice;
- placing the right toe pick onto the ice too close to the left foot.

Lunging forward on the take-off is caused by:

- not arching the back;
- lowering the chin;
- looking down;
- commencing the right arm motion from a position to the side of the body

instead of straight back and pointing in the direction in which you are skating (this means that the arm must pass on an arc that is downward and in front of the body during the take-off, increasing the probability of bending forward at the waist).

As I mentioned at the beginning, the overall direction of movement for the flip jump is a straight line. The most common deviation from this direction can occur on the left back inside take-off edge. If the edge has much of a curve to it, you should suspect that you may be leaning in too far.

A second problem that can be discerned by examining the imprint on the ice is the relationship of the toe-pick mark to the take-off edge. If these are more than one foot apart, you should suspect that your free leg has swung on the three-turn, ending up too far to the inside of the take-off edge prior to the toe-assist action. This can also indicate that the shoulders were not parallel to the skating foot, but were overrotated when the lift-off motion was initiated.

THE LUTZ

The Lutz jump is unique; there is no edge jump that is equivalent to it. In addition, like the Walley and the toe Walley, the rotation in the air during the Lutz is in the opposite direction to the inherent rotation of the take-off edge.

The Lutz consists of a left back outside take-off edge with a right toe-pick assist, one counterclockwise revolution in the air, and a landing on a right back outside edge. Alois Lutz, a member of the Viennese Skating Club before World War II, invented this spectacular jump, and it has been a staple of figure skating ever since.

The Preparation:

The preparation for the Lutz is quite different from most other jump preparations. Skate back crossovers clockwise around the side of the rink. The preparation and take-off edge are the same: a left back outside edge. When you are in the center part of the rink and are skating toward the end, start the preparation. Step onto the left back outside edge so that the heel of the left foot is pointing toward the end of the rink.

The Windup:

The first part of the take-off edge constitutes the preparatory phase of the take-off. As you step onto the left back outside edge, your left arm and shoulder should be back and your right arm and shoulder in front of you. You should be looking back and to the inside.

Once you've shifted your weight to the left foot, and are in the process of lifting your right foot off the ice in front of you, turn your head clockwise. You will now be looking over your right shoulder. The movement of the head will cause your shoulders to move into a position that creates a line perpendicular to the skating foot. However, keep your right arm extended in front of you. Your left arm will be out to the side. In this position, extend your right leg with your right foot about two feet in front of the left. Stand on a straight left knee.

In this position, you will be looking over the right shoulder, in the direction in which you are skating. The edge should curve around gently, meaning that you should be leaning into the circle just slightly. When the edge is just about parallel to a line running across the width of the rink, it is time to begin the preparation for the lift-off.

To prepare for the lift-off, you must execute several movements simultaneously. Move your right arm, shoulder, and leg back. The movement of your right arm should be close to the body and should stop when it is pointing in the direction in which you are skating. The right leg should pass close to the left leg and extend straight back, close to the ice. Once the right leg has passed the left, bend the left leg deeply in preparation for the spring. Turn your head slowly until you are looking back in the direction from which you have come. Your left arm will be straight in front of you. During this process, the imprint on the ice will begin to assume a slightly tighter curve, until you are skating more or less across the width of the rink.

The Take-Off:

To initiate the lift-off, place the right toe pick in the ice and spring from the left leg. Move your arms in a walking motion, using the same technique employed on the lift-off for the flip jump: as you leave the ice, your left arm will be back and your right arm in front. Your shoulders will rotate counterclockwise to a position nearly parallel with the skating foot. As your arms and shoulders rotate, turn your head counterclockwise until you are looking over your left shoulder. Although the rotation of your upper body is counterclockwise and contrary to the inherent rotational direction of the edge, which is clockwise, it will have sufficient force to cause the edge to curve more. Be careful that it doesn't curve too much. The last few inches of the edge should produce a line that forms about a 75-degree angle with the side of the rink.

Once in the air, retract your arms and legs into the conventional rotating position. The preparation for the landing and the landing itself are executed in the usual way.

The key to the Lutz is the timing of the movements and the control of the rotational forces. Throughout the preparation, it is essential to control the rotation, which tends to move in the clockwise direction as determined by the preparatory/take-off edge. When the right leg, arm, and shoulder rotate clockwise, the head counteracts this by moving counterclockwise. The strong and rapid counterclockwise movements of the arms, shoulders, and head on the lift-off are tempered—not negated—by the placement of the right toe in the ice. All of the opposing forces throughout the take-off establish the dynamics necessary to execute a successful Lutz.

The ideal imprint on the ice was mentioned throughout the description because it is such an essential part of the technique for the Lutz. As always, deviations in the imprint indicate technical errors.

- If the edge is curved during the first part of the preparation, it means that you are leaning too far into the circle. This will add additional force to the inherent rotational momentum of the take-off edge, which can prevent you from controlling the rotation in that direction and from achieving the proper counterclockwise rotation required for a satisfactory take-off.
- A change of edge immediately prior to lift-off means that your upper body has rotated too far before leaving the ice or that you have dropped your right shoulder and hip. In either case, you will not have executed a Lutz jump but rather will have performed a flip.
- An excessively curved line for the take-off edge during the last phase of the preparation, or during the lift-off, means that you are leaning too far into the circle. This makes it difficult to control the inherent clockwise rotation of the take-off edge.

A

B

C

H

I

The Lutz

Here, Brian Boitano demonstrates a double Lutz. When performing any Lutz, start by skating back crossovers clockwise around the rink (A). On the first part of the preparation for the take-off, look over your right shoulder, keeping your arms relaxed (B). As you reach back with your right leg and arm for the take-off, look forward. As you are about to place your right toe pick on the ice, your edge will begin to curve more deeply (C). On the take-off, pass your left arm and shoulder back and your right arm and shoulder forward (D). Once in the air, retract your arms and legs in the conventional rotating position (E). After two counterclockwise revolutions (F), land in the usual way (G, H, I).

D   E   F   G

Pattern followed for a Lutz jump.

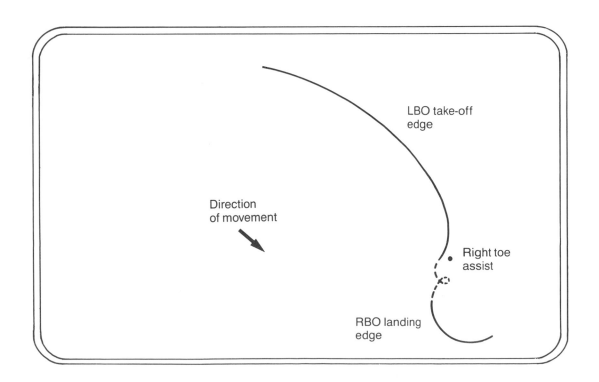

LBO take-off edge

Direction of movement

Right toe assist

RBO landing edge

The Double Lutz

The double Lutz is merely a single Lutz with one additional revolution in the air.

The Triple Lutz

The triple Lutz was first performed in competition by Donald Jackson of Canada at the 1962 World Championships, when it represented the first toe-assisted triple ever executed in a major international competition. It is a double Lutz with one additional revolution in the air.

Common Errors When Performing the Lutz

A landing in which the body is leaning too far into the circle of the landing edge, perhaps even causing a fall, is caused by:

- dropping the right shoulder on the lift-off;
- swinging the arms around on the lift-off;
- bending forward during the final stage of the preparation and on the take-off.

A low jump is caused by:

- overrotation of the upper body on the lift-off;
- excessive clockwise rotational momentum on the preparation;
- poor timing on the preparation and take-off;
- slow spring from the left leg.

Collapse of the right foot at the ankle during lift-off is caused by overrotation of the upper body on the lift-off.

Overrotation of the upper body on the lift-off is caused by:

- passing the arms around instead of close to the body on the lift-off;
- turning the head over the left shoulder too early during the lift-off motion;
- allowing the right arm and shoulder to begin moving forward in anticipation of the lift-off;
- the arms moving around instead of close to the body on the windup.

THE REVERSE DOUBLE LUTZ

In 1968 I invented a variation of the Lutz jump that has never been performed in competition and, to my knowledge, has never been performed by any other skater. It consists of a Lutz take-off, one and a half counterclockwise revolutions in the air, and a landing on the right forward outside edge with a left toe-pick assist. The intriguing aspect of this jump is that the take-off and the landing are on the same circle, rotating clockwise, while the turns in the air are counterclockwise. This juxtaposition of the direction of rotation in the air with the direction of rotation on the take-off and landing edges, creating the only jump with a bracket-like motion, produces an exciting effect.

The key differences between an ordinary double Lutz jump and the reverse double Lutz are the preparation for the landing and the landing itself. Since the landing edge has a direction of rotation opposite to the direction of rotation in the air, it is essential to prepare earlier than usual for the landing. This means that you must slow the rotation by opening your arms out to the side after only one revolution in the air. The first point of touchdown should be the left toe pick. A split second later, you place your right foot on the ice, on a right forward outside edge. During the touchdown, thrust your left arm forward and your right arm to the side to stop the rotation. Lean toward the right shoulder.

This jump is not particularly difficult, provided that you have sufficient time in the air to prepare for the landing—which means that it must be a relatively high jump. In addition, it is helpful to execute the arm motion on the take-off with greater ease, that is less vigorously, than normal. Nonetheless, the strength of the check in the landing and the early preparation for the landing are the keys to this jump.

Pattern followed for a reverse Lutz.

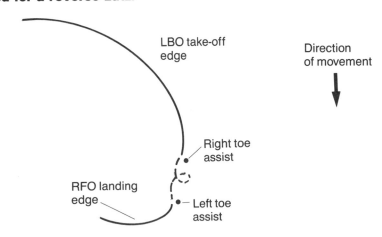

LBO take-off edge

Direction of movement

Right toe assist

RFO landing edge

Left toe assist

16

Splits and Stags

Splits and stags rightfully belong in the category of toe-assisted jumps. However, it is useful to discuss them separately, since the principles of the jump following the take-off are quite different. In addition, they are not fundamentally rotational jumps but rather positional jumps; that is, the objective is a beautiful or creative position in the air. On the other hand, the techniques already discussed in Chapter 15 apply, up to the point at which you leave the ice.

THE SPLIT JUMP

The split jump consists of a flip jump take-off, a half revolution in the air, a split position in the air, and a landing on a right forward inside edge with a left toe-pick assist.

The easiest way to enter the take-off edge, which is a left back inside edge, is with a forward inside Mohawk: a right forward inside edge with a change onto a left back inside edge. Following the Mohawk, the technique is the same as that employed on the flip jump.

On the lift-off, you must begin to prepare for the split position. If you have properly executed the preparation and take-off movements, the half revolution will occur automatically during the transition from the lift-off to the split position. As you leave the ice, reach forward with your left leg and back with your right. Both legs should be turned out with the toes pointed; this will require more effort on the right leg. Both legs should be straight and locked in that position. Keep the arms out to the side.

The split position produces a spectacular impression when the legs form

A split jump is always a spectacular part of any program.

The split jump.
A good split position consists of straight legs turned out, with pointed toes. Arch your back and keep your shoulders down.

a straight line parallel to your line of flight and to the ice, when your back is arched and your chin is up, and when your arms are straight out to the side.

Touchdown first occurs with the left toe pick, followed immediately by the placement of the right foot on a forward inside edge. The left foot essentially breaks most of the downward force on the landing and provides almost a push-off motion as the weight is transferred completely to a bent right leg. The left arm should move forward, while the right arm should remain to the side. In fact, you may wish to place a certain amount of forward pressure on the left arm to the extent necessary to break the rotation.

THE STAG JUMP

The stag jump is a simple variation on the split jump. Instead of extending the left leg straight out in front for the split position in the air, the left leg is held in a bent position in front. The one important difference relates to the manner in which you bend the left leg. The ideal position consists of the following:

- the right leg is back, in the position it would be in for an ordinary split jump;
- the left thigh—from the hip to the knee—is also in a split position; and
- the left knee is fully bent, so that the left calf is touching the hamstrings.

In my opinion, the stag is far less dramatic than the split, but far more showy.

The stag jump.
On the stag, bend the left leg in front by raising your left knee.

THE RUSSIAN SPLIT JUMP

The only difference between the split and the Russian split is the position in the air. When doing the Russian split, you want to be in a sitting position with your legs straight out, open as wide as possible. It is not necessary to adopt an open hip position, but it is essential to point the toes. One other feature of the Russian split is that you must touch your toes with your hands in the middle of the jump. This is not as difficult as you might think. The only difficulty is keeping your back arched, chin up, and shoulders in a relaxed position as you reach for your toes. The rest of the technique is the same as that employed on the split jump.

The Russian split can be one of the more dramatic and rousing jumps. I can recall the sensation of jumping well above the hockey boards on this jump and being able to look down on the first row of spectators! Both you and the spectator can derive great pleasure from a well-executed Russian split.

THE RUSSIAN SPLIT FLIP

The preparation and take-off on the Russian split flip are the same as for the ordinary Russian split jump. The only difference is that an additional half revolution is added after the Russian split position in the air, resulting in a landing on a right back outside edge. This addition, however, is not trivial. It means that you must assume the Russian split position more quickly following the lift-off, and that, from the Russian split position, you must quickly drop your legs and contract your arms into the rotating position. In addition, the check to stop the rotation as you land must be quite strong.

The Russian split position.

Three subtleties are worth noting: 1) The Russian split position must be completed immediately prior to reaching the peak of the jump, allowing you to move to the rotational position; 2) the rotational position will not be as tight or as refined as the position required for most rotational jumps; and 3) the rotation must be completed prior to the landing, to allow you sufficient time to brake the rotation before landing by opening the arms into the check position.

THE RUSSIAN SPLIT LUTZ

The Russian split Lutz is exactly what the name implies: a Russian split in the context of a Lutz jump. It is similar in all aspects to the Russian split flip except that the take-off is the same as a Lutz jump take-off. Because of the change in rotational direction during the jump—from the clockwise direction of the take-off edge to the counterclockwise direction of the rotation in the air and the landing edge—the Russian split Lutz is slightly more interesting to watch than a Russian split flip. It is worth learning.

THE BOURKEY

The Bourkey, named after my coach, is a very unusual jump that I invented in 1966. While it is not as spectacular as a Russian split, it is unusual in position and intriguing in motion. It is not an easy maneuver, requiring substantial height on the jump and split-second timing in preparation for the landing.

The Bourkey consists of an ordinary split jump preparation and take-off, half a revolution prior to the position in the air, followed by half a revolution in preparation for the landing, and a landing on a right back outside edge. It is essentially a flip jump with a Bourkey position in the air.

The Bourkey.
Very few skaters have achieved competence in the Bourkey. Here, the author performing a Bourkey in 1966.

The unusual aspect of this jump is the Bourkey position in the air. To assume the Bourkey position, extend the left leg out to the side following the take-off. Bend the right leg and simultaneously bring the right foot up so that it touches the left thigh. This leg motion will tend to tilt your body to the right. To counteract this, extend the left arm to the side, parallel with the left leg. Bend the right arm in front of the chest, pointing it toward the left hand. (The right arm virtually mimics the position of the right leg, while the left arm mimics the position of the left leg.) Look to the left, and keep your back arched. As in the case of a Russian split flip, this position must be achieved just prior to the peak of the jump.

What makes the position in the air unusual is that the right leg is essentially in front of the left, the reverse of the conventional rotating position for a counterclockwise jump. To come out of the Bourkey position, the legs must return to the conventional position. This means that as both legs move down into the rotating position, the right moves behind the left. In addition, since the arms are already fully rotated in the direction of the rotation, the contraction into the rotating position essentially moves opposite to the rotation. Fortunately, the take-off and the mere contraction of the arms will create sufficient rotational momentum to counteract the direction of the arm movement and to accomplish the final half revolution. The unique changes in arm and leg position on this jump result in its unusual appearance. The preparation for the landing and the landing itself are the same as those employed on the split flip.

Needless to say, this jump is quite different and difficult, and it deserves more common practice than it currently enjoys.

17

Jump Combinations

The number of possible jump combinations is limitless, at least in practical terms. If a change of feet or a turn is permitted between the jumps, any sequence of jumps is possible. On the other hand, if the landing of one jump is the take-off for the next one—as in a sequence of loop jumps—the landing will dictate the possibilities for the next jump.

For example, if you land on the usual right back outside edge, the only jumps available without a change of feet or a turn are the loop, the toe loop, the Walley, and the toe Walley, the latter two requiring only a change of edge. If a change of foot or a turn is permitted, the Axel, Salchow, flip, Lutz, inside Axel, and the position jumps are added to your options.

While many different combinations are possible, two general principles govern all combinations. Therefore I shall describe those, along with one or two examples, and leave the creation of the combinations to you.

Not surprisingly, the most important principle relates to rotation. Rotational momentum tends to build in the context of a jump sequence. The trick is to control it on the landings, without checking the landing so hard that no momentum is available for the next jump. If rotation is not controlled, overrotation on subsequent jumps will cause them to fail.

The method by which you control the rotation differs according to the nature of the landing and take-off edges. The two parts of the body whose positions you can alter dramatically are the arms and the free leg. The arms regulate the shoulders and upper body position, while the free leg dictates the positioning of the hips. Both contribute to the curvature of the edge. On an Axel / double toe loop combination, it is the clockwise check of the arms on the landing (which is the preparatory windup for the double toe loop) that controls the rotation. On the one-foot Axel / double flip, it is both the clock-

271

The trick in performing jump combinations is to control rotation without sacrificing momentum for the next jump.

wise check of the arms and the extension of the free leg back on the landing that stops the rotation in preparation for the double flip take-off. If your technique on the basic jumps is solid, and if you understand the principles of those jumps, the methods for controlling the rotation will be obvious.

An example of this was covered in the loop jump sequence (see page 226). Another example, with slightly different dynamics, is the Axel / double toe loop combination. In this case, the check on the landing of the Axel must be strong enough to allow you to adopt the preparatory position for the take-off for the double toe loop—prior to the actual take-off. This requires a slightly different approach from that used on the loop jump sequence.

The underlying message, then, is that the subsequent jump governs the technique employed to control the rotation on the landing of the preceding jump.

The second important principle has to do with the relationship between the landing on the first jump and the spring into the next jump. On the landing, the landing leg bends to cushion the downward force of the jump. If the take-off for the next jump is immediate, as is the case in an Axel / double toe loop combination or in an Axel / double loop combination, the bend on the landing is the preparation for the spring on the take-off. On the other hand, if some time elapses between the jumps, and if a series of movements occur to prepare for the subsequent jump, the leg bend for the spring may be separated from the bend on the landing by a slight straightening of the skating leg. This will pertain, for example, to the one-foot Axel / double Salchow combination.

While the variety of possible jump combinations is enormous, here are a number of the more common combinations, in this case with an immediate take-off after landing (recall that edge jumps designated by the term "half" are landed on the left back inside edge):

> Axel / half loop / Salchow / toe loop
> Axel / half loop / Salchow / loop
> One-foot Axel / Salchow / toe loop / loop
> Axel / half loop / flip / loop

A few examples with turns or changes of feet between jumps (recall that toe-assisted jumps designated by the term "half" consist of a half revolution with a toe-assisted landing):

> Half flip / left forward outside three-turn / flip /
> loop / right back outside three-turn /
> counterclockwise inside Mohawk / Salchow

Half flip / left forward outside three-turn / one-foot Salchow / left back inside three-turn / Axel

Half toe loop / right forward inside three-turn / toe loop / loop

Split jump / right forward inside three-turn / toe loop / half loop / Salchow

18

Pairs and Ice Dancing

PAIRS

Although skating aficionados frequently refer to pair skating as a more acrobatic form of single skating performed by a man and a woman simultaneously—a technically accurate description—pairs is much, much more. In addition to the maneuvers characteristic of single free skating—jumps, spins, and footwork—other elements such as lifts and spins, throw maneuvers, pull spin maneuvers, interactive choreography, unision, and communication constitute additional aspects of pair skating. These make pairs more exacting and difficult than single free skating. When these technical elements are coupled with the importance and inherent subtleties of the relationship between the two members of a pair team, the level of complexity is increased further. Despite these hurdles, pair skating can be one of the most rewarding and thrilling disciplines in figure skating.

One of the most important issues, which requires careful consideration at the outset, is the choice of a partner. Some of the key points that must be evaluated are:

1. *Physical characteristics:* This is a technical consideration and bears directly on your ability to succeed. The man should be slightly taller than the woman. However, if he is too much taller (six inches, for example), some of the harmony of the pair can be lost. This unfortunately has been particularly noticeable in some of the recent pair teams. The woman should be strong but not too hefty or stout. Additional weight from a large skeletal structure or an over-muscled body makes the man's task exponentially more difficult.

2. Both skaters should have developed or be capable of developing *solid expertise in single's free skating.* In order to be competitive, pair skaters are

275

Irina Rodnina and Alexsandr Zaitsev: perfectly matched
for pairs skating.

required by the rules to execute difficult single free-skating maneuvers precisely. In addition, solid skating skills make pair skating easier and remove some of the risk of injury, particularly for the woman.

3. Both individuals should recognize and accept that pair skating is a *long-term commitment* to their partner and to skating. While it is possible to change partners at various points in a skating career, it is far from ideal, and realistically will probably preclude you from reaching the pinnacle of your potential. Forethought is a priceless treasure; afterthought is a cheap commodity.

4. *Compatibility* is important. Having a pair partner is almost as close a relationship as having a husband or a wife. You will spend an extraordinary amount of time with your partner. If fundamental differences in outlook, personality, or "chemistry" exist, chances are that you face a rough passage in the future, when pressure and intensity reach new heights. Honesty with yourself and with your partner can circumvent a lot of future hardships. Too, you should remember, perhaps above all else, that your relationship with your partner is a professional relationship.

These represent only the most critical issues to consider when choosing a pair partner. If you are matched with a partner when you are young, or if you are paired with a brother or a sister by virtue of convenience, some of these considerations will be difficult or impossible to assess. Compromising on various issues may represent the best strategy as you proceed down your skating career paths.

The number of elements specific to pair skating has mushroomed over the past 20 years, and a discussion of the techniques for all these would require a separate book. However, it is worth noting some of the more common maneuvers. These can be categorized into pair spins, death spirals, pair lifts, throw jumps, and solo spins. (This excludes all single maneuvers in which the skaters execute the move without depending on the partner, such as side-by-side jumps.)

Pair Spins

The most common pair spins are pair sit spins, camels, and flying camels. The *pair sit spin* is often approached from back crossovers in the clockwise direction. The skaters step toward each other on the entrance edge, and end up facing each other while spinning in a sit spin position. It is important to note that the technically correct way of executing a sit spin must give way to a freer form: a pair sit spin requires a hunched back position and a fully bent skating leg.

A *pair camel* spin requires that the skaters spin side by side, with the man holding the woman. As in the pair sit spin, the pair camel is approached from clockwise back crossovers and is entered by the skaters' stepping toward each other. In this spin, however, the woman nearly comes to a stop on the entrance edge. The rotational momentum for the spin is created by the man, who executes the entrance three-turn just prior to coming into contact with the woman. The force of his movements creates the spin.

The *pair flying camel* is a poor second cousin to the single's flying camel. Because the skaters are jumping toward each other, the maximum rotational force cannot be generated in this case. The step-over is subdued; you must surrender rotational force for the correct performance (placement) of the back camel spin relative to your partner. During the back camel, each partner faces the foot of the other.

Death Spirals

The death spiral is one of the more elegant pair moves, combining the fluidity of skating with the drama of acrobatics. Basically, the man slowly enters a pivot, a particular type of two-foot spin that consists of a spin on one toe and an edge on the other skate. It is the only example of a toe-assisted spin in skating. The woman, who clasps the man's hand, is pulled around in the spin. The unique feature of this spin is that she ultimately is moving in a large circle around him, horizontal to the ice. In fact, her head occasionally skims the surface of the ice. Death spirals are defined by the direction in which the woman is going and by the edge on which she is skating. There are forward and backward, outside and inside death spirals.

Pair Lifts

Many different types of pair lifts are possible. The way in which you approach the lift, the way the man lifts the woman into the air, and the position of the woman in the air define each lift. Some lifts, such as those involving holding the woman's legs, a horizontal position of the woman in the air, or extended carrying of the partner around the ice, are forbidden in amateur competition. The most common lifts are the overhead, the lasso, the star, the press lift, the loop waist lift, and the split double Lutz twist.

The *overhead hand-to-hand press* lift requires that the skaters approach the

Pairs Skating

Strength, technique, and caution
are essential when attempting any
pairs lift.

The death spiral: one of the more
elegant moves in pairs skating.

lift face-to-face, the woman skating backward and the man skating forward. The man essentially presses the woman into an overhead position in front of him, the arms of both skaters being fully extended. The woman leaves the ice from two feet and turns one to two and a half revolutions in the air, landing on a back outside edge.

The *lasso,* also an overhead lift, is just what the name suggests: a lift involving a lasso-like motion as the man lifts the woman. Both individuals skate forward, side-by-side. The man's right arm is over the woman's head, right hand to right hand. The man holds the woman's left hand in his left. On the lift-off, the woman basically jumps from a left forward outside edge while the man swings her around and up behind him. In the air, the woman will be behind the man, the arms of both partners fully extended. She will land on a back outside edge after one and a half to two and a half revolutions in the air.

The *toe lasso* lift is like the regular lasso except that on the entrance, the man skates forward and the woman skates backward. Since the woman is lifting off from a back edge, she will rotate only one to two revolutions in the air.

In the *star* lift, the man lifts the woman with one hand on her waist and the other in a hand-to-hand position—his left holding her right. Both skaters enter the lift skating backward. In the air, the woman is essentially horizontal and on her side. The position of her legs is variable and open to substantial creativity. By releasing the hand-to-hand position, the man can hold his partner in the air with only one hand.

The *hand-to-hand loop* lift, sometimes referred to as a "press" lift, is one in which the man lifts the woman into what is essentially a loop jump. In preparation for this lift, the woman is in front of the man, both skating backward. A slight variation on this lift is a *loop waist* lift, which requires the man to lift the woman by holding on to her waist.

The *split double twist* is a true combination of a single's jump with a pair lift. Both skaters execute back crossovers as if to approach a double Lutz. The woman is in front of the man, who grasps her by the waist in preparation for the lift. He lifts her into a split position and then lets go of her as she rotates the two revolutions in the air. Just prior to her feet hitting the ice, he grasps her by the waist to break the force of the landing.

There are many other lifts as well as variations of these common lifts. A *lateral* lift, in which the woman rotates horizontally in the air above the man's head, is a variation on a star lift. The *"bucket"* is an exit from an overhead lift. Numerous variations, some observed only once in competition, have been invented. You, the skater, along with your coach should take the initiative to create new moves.

One fundamental principle pertains to all pair lifts (as well as to throws, which are discussed below): Both skaters must contribute to the lift-off. The woman does this by springing off the ice. The man assists by bending and straightening his knees in concert with the woman. This establishes the upward momentum, which is continued by the straightening of the man's arms.

Throw Jumps

A throw jump is a single jump executed by the woman with the man enhancing the upward and outward momentum by carefully throwing the woman into the jump. While every single's jump can be turned into a throw, the most common are the throw Axel or double Axel, the throw double or triple Salchow, the throw double or triple toe loop, and the throw double or triple loop. The techniques for accomplishing a throw are essentially the same as those for executing the single's jump. The principal difference is that the man, skating backward, helps to control the rotational momentum on the take-off and enables the woman to achieve great height and distance on the jump. Russian pair teams tend to emphasize distance rather than height to reduce the chance of serious injury to the woman.

Side-by-Side Spins

Pairs can execute solo spins side by side. The only reason to mention these separately is to make note of one important objective: Ideally, the revolutions of the two skaters should be synchronous. This applies to all spins except fast-forward and -backward upright spins, and cross-foot spins, in which the rotations are too fast to ascertain whether or not synchronization has been achieved.

ICE DANCING

Ice dancing represents the most elegant and sophisticated of the disciplines of figure skating. It is every bit as athletic as singles and pair skating but requires different skills. Ice dancers must be agile and quick, and must possess strong legs and backs. In ice dancing, athleticism is, in the strictest sense, the servant of beauty.

Although ice dancing has become particularly prominent recently, largely as a result of the enormous contribution made by the 1984 Olympic Gold

With their gold-winning performance in the 1984 Olympics, Jayne Torvill and Christopher Dean brought new prominence to ice dancing.

Natalia Bestemianova and Andrei Bukin: two of the world's great ice dancers.

Medalists Jayne Torvill and Christopher Dean, it has had a slow development historically. Its origins date back to the nineteenth century, but its rapid evolution became possible only in the 1970s when 1) more attention was focused on the free dance routine, 2) a new compulsory dance was added, the original set pattern dance, which allowed dancers to create their own set pattern dance, and 3) ice dancing became an Olympic event, in 1976. The confluence of these changes created an environment in which innovation flourished, making ice dancing one of the most interesting and appealing disciplines of modern figure skating.

Ice dancing consists of footwork sequences, positional moves, position changes, and small lifts and spins which serve to accentuate the choreography and the element of the "dance." Many restrictions apply to ice dancing, the rationale for which is the attempt to prevent ice dancing from becoming pair skating. At the root of these restrictions is the requirement for ice dancing to be just that, a dance. For this reason, aficionados demand that the free dance programs of ice dancers possess a specific dance rhythm—waltz, tango, foxtrot, rumba, even rock-and-roll. Not surprisingly, this theory has been ignored quite successfully by many dancers, including Torvill and Dean. The argument against a rigid interpretation of the dance as having a traditional ballroom rhythm is that dancing continues to evolve, adding new rhythms and approaches. A Broadway show tune for which a particular dance was originally conceived is as much a dance as is the waltz. Both schools of thought persist, the prevailing one being determined by the philosophy of the best ice dancers at any one time.

In ice dancing, the basic elements of figure skating are of paramount importance: edges, pointed toes, proper posture, smooth turns, and fluidity. In addition, smooth position changes and synchronization are critical. Overriding all these elements is the fundamental requirement of musical interpretation and creative, yet appropriate, choreography.

19

The Program/
The "Great" Skater

THE PROGRAM

The final objective of learning the technical elements of figure skating is to bring them all together in a coherent whole: the program. In the context of a program, the music and choreography breathe life into the isolated elements; each move and each movement take on new meaning and significance. The skater's goal enlarges from merely executing a move successfully to creating a compelling and unique experience. Perfect technique provides the springboard from which you can leap to this new level.

A skater's program consists of the technical elements of skating assembled in a defined order more or less dictated by the music. In amateur competition, the length of the program is defined and is determined by the level of the skater. At the Senior level, the Men's Singles and Pairs skate four and a half minutes, whereas the Ladies' Singles and Ice Dancers skate four minutes. The skater chooses the music, although some restrictions apply. For example, vocal music is not permitted in amateur competition.

Once you have chosen the music, you can begin to choreograph your program. It is important to define a point of view before beginning to compile the program. This can be as unstructured as stringing together a series of unrelated movements or as structured as telling a story. Regardless of the nature of the point of view, the approach must be conscious. This will ensure that all of the movements will serve a single purpose and therefore will have meaning. No move should occur without a purpose, and at no time during the program should the skater be inactive, unless for a specific reason.

When putting the elements together, it is essential to allow the music and the point of view to determine when and where to execute a particular move,

285

Once you've learned the technical elements of skating, the next step is putting them all together into a program.

and how the move should be executed. Regrettably, skaters often address technical demands first and assemble the program on the basis of their technical objectives. If you are sufficiently competent, this method will not prevail, except for the most difficult of moves. In addition, the moves must serve as the messenger of the music and the point of view. In other words, you must interpret the music.

Once the program is set, you must practice it repeatedly. This is necessary for several reasons: 1) The sequence of the moves must become second nature; 2) the technical hurdles must be overcome in the context of the program; 3) you must build stamina; and 4) you must be able to perform your program so well that your only thought in a performance is to create the desired effect, the experience.

To enhance the program, it is helpful to wear an outfit that is consistent with the music and the point of view. For example, if you are skating to Spanish music, a costume with a Spanish flair would be appropriate. The costume enhances the meaning.

The consummate program is fundamentally one in which the experience transcends the technical excellence. This requires perfect technique which, for the skater, must be automatic. Virtually the only thought in your mind is the creation of the experience—the musicality and the expression of the point of view must overwhelm both the skater and the observer. When this happens, you will create a magical moment. I had the good fortune of creating such moments at the 1968 National Championships and at many exhibitions during the last two years of my career, when I skated a special program to "Somewhere" from Leonard Bernstein's *West Side Story*. Believe me, creating a magical moment is an unforgettable experience, one that every committed skater ultimately strives for.

THE "GREAT" SKATER

To become a "great" skater is a goal achieved by very few, but one worth aiming for. A great skater is one who changes the sport by being in it, a person who makes a contribution that alters the course of skating history. As a result of that person's participation, the sport changes in some significant way.

There are many ways in which this can occur. However, the hallmark of a great skater is superlative technique coupled with the ability to transcend that technique and create something unique and excellent. A few of the great skaters of the past are Dick Button, who brought athleticism to new, unheard-of

Creating a magical moment on the ice is what every skater strives for in a free program.

heights; the Protopovs, who brought the element of ballet and artistry to pairs; Janet Lynn, who created a pure synthesis of musicality, grace, and athleticism; and Torvill and Dean, who brought a harmony of purpose and movement to ice dancing. This is but a short list.

Commitment, creativity, musicality, a point of view, and superlative technique are the elements required to achieve greatness. However, this task cannot be accomplished without the one fundamental element: the love of skating. The goal is worth pursuing. Perhaps someday you too will be ranked with the great skaters of the past.